OTHER PUBLICATIONS FROM THE DRUCKER FOUNDATION

Organizational Leadership Resource

The Drucker Foundation Self-Assessment Tool

The Drucker Foundation Future Series

The Leader of the Future, *Frances Hesselbein, Marshall Goldsmith, Richard Beckhard, Editors*

The Organization of the Future, *Frances Hesselbein, Marshall Goldsmith, Richard Beckhard, Editors*

The Community of the Future, *Frances Hesselbein, Marshall Goldsmith, Richard Beckhard, Richard F. Schubert, Editors*

Wisdom to Action Series

Leading for Innovation, *Frances Hesselbein, Marshall Goldsmith, Iain Somerville, Editors*

Leading Beyond the Walls, *Frances Hesselbein, Marshall Goldsmith, Iain Somerville, Editors*

Leaderbooks

The Collaboration Challenge: How Nonprofits and Businesses Succeed Through Strategic Alliances, *James E. Austin*

Meeting the Collaboration Challenge (workbook and video)

Journal and Related Books

Leader to Leader Journal

Leader to Leader: Enduring Insights on Leadership from the Drucker Foundation's Award-Winning Journal, *Frances Hesselbein, Paul Cohen, Editors*

On High-Performance Organizations, *Frances Hesselbein, Rob Johnston, Editors*

On Leading Change, *Frances Hesselbein, Rob Johnston, Editors*

On Mission and Leadership, *Frances Hesselbein, Rob Johnston, Editors*

Video Training Resources

Excellence in Nonprofit Leadership Video, *featuring Peter F. Drucker, Max De Pree, Frances Hesselbein, and Michele Hunt. Moderated by Richard F. Schubert*

Leading in a Time of Change: What It Will Take to Lead Tomorrow, *a conversation with Peter F. Drucker and Peter M. Senge, introduction by Frances Hesselbein*

Lessons in Leadership Video, *with Peter F. Drucker*

Online Resources

www.drucker.org

On High-Performance Organizations

A DRUCKER FOUNDATION
LEADERBOOK

ABOUT THE DRUCKER FOUNDATION

The Peter F. Drucker Foundation for Nonprofit Management, founded in 1990, takes its name and inspiration from the acknowledged father of modern management. By providing educational opportunities and resources, the foundation furthers its mission "to lead social sector organizations toward excellence in performance." It pursues this mission through the presentation of conferences, video teleconferences, the annual Peter F. Drucker Award for Nonprofit Innovation, and the annual Frances Hesselbein Community Innovation Fellows Program, as well as through the development of management resources, partnerships, and publications.

The Drucker Foundation believes that a healthy society requires three vital sectors: a public sector of effective governments, a private sector of effective businesses, and a social sector of effective community organizations. The mission of the social sector and its organizations is to change lives. It accomplishes this mission by addressing the needs of the spirit, mind, and body of individuals, the community, and society. This sector and its organizations also create a meaningful sphere of effective and responsible citizenship.

In the ten years after its inception, the Drucker Foundation, among other things:

- Presented the Drucker Innovation Award, which each year generates hundreds of applications from local community enterprises; many applicants work in fields in which results are difficult to achieve

- Worked with social sector leaders through the Frances Hesselbein Community Innovation Fellows program

- Held more than twenty conferences in the United States and in countries around the world

- Developed thirteen books: the *Self-Assessment Tool* (revised 1998), for nonprofit organizations; three books in the Drucker Foundation Future Series, *The Leader of the Future* (1996), *The Organization of the Future* (1997), and *The Community of the Future* (1998); *Leader to Leader* (1999); *Leading Beyond the Walls* (1999); *The Collaboration Challenge* (2000); the *Leading in a Time of Change* viewer's workbook and video (2001); *Leading for Innovation* (2002); and *On Mission and Leadership, On Leading Change, On High-Performance Organizations,* and *On Creativity, Innovation, and Renewal* (all 2002)

- Developed *Leader to Leader,* a quarterly journal for leaders from all three sectors

- Established a Web site (drucker.org) that shares articles on leadership and management and examples of nonprofit innovation with hundreds of thousands of visitors each year

For more information on the Drucker Foundation, contact:

The Peter F. Drucker Foundation for Nonprofit Management
320 Park Avenue, Third Floor, New York, NY 10022-6839 U.S.A.
Telephone: (212) 224-1174 • Fax: (212) 224-2508
E-mail: info@pfdf.org • Web address: www.drucker.org

On High-Performance Organizations

A Leader to Leader Guide

Frances Hesselbein
Rob Johnston
Editors

JOSSEY-BASS
A Wiley Company
www.josseybass.com

Published by

JOSSEY-BASS
A Wiley Company
989 Market Street
San Francisco, CA 94103-1741

www.josseybass.com

Jossey-Bass books and products are available through most bookstores. To contact Jossey-Bass directly, call (888) 378-2537, fax to (800) 605-2665, or visit our Web site at www.josseybass.com.

Substantial discounts on bulk quantities of Jossey-Bass books are available to corporations, professional associations, and other organizations. For details and discount information, contact the special sales department at Jossey-Bass.

We at Jossey-Bass strive to use the most environmentally sensitive paper stocks available to us. Our publications are printed on acid-free recycled stock whenever possible, and our paper always meets or exceeds minimum GPO and EPA requirements.

Library of Congress Cataloging-in-Publication Data

On high-performance organizations : a leader to leader guide / Frances Hesselbein and Rob Johnston, editors.-1st ed.
 p. cm.
"Drucker Foundation Leaderbooks."
Includes index.
ISBN 0-7879-6069-1 (alk. paper)
 1. Organizational effectiveness 2. Organizational change. 3. Leadership. I. Hesselbein, Frances. II. Johnston, Rob, date
HD58.9 .O54 2002
658.4-dc21   2001007587

FIRST EDITION

HB Printing 10 9 8 7 6 5 4 3 2 1

Contents

Introduction

People in the United States and around the world have an enormous hunger for ideas; that's why in 1996 the Drucker Foundation launched *Leader to Leader*, a journal of ideas by leaders for leaders. This hunger among millions of working executives demonstrates their concern for the future and commitment to making a difference.

The incisive thinkers and remarkable leaders who have contributed to the journal and its related books open doors, spark ideas, raise signal flags, and help satisfy that universal hunger. These extraordinary contributors have taught us, among other things, that great leaders do not live isolated from the world; they are engaged with and deeply care about others. They measure their own success by the real-world impact of their work. That people throughout our society and organizations want to contribute to a better world has been a major premise of *Leader to Leader*.

We learned, too, that astonishing things happen when you give intelligent, effective people a free hand. Never have we approached our authors with an assigned topic or reviewed their work before an advisory board or peer review; when you're working with the best in the world, you don't do that. Rather, we simply asked, "What's on your mind? What issues will most affect leaders, organizations, or communities in the coming years?"

From that unfettered process, several coherent themes emerged with astonishing clarity. They are evident in the four volumes of the Leader to Leader Guides. This volume, *On High-Performance Organizations*, explores getting the most from the people and other resources of each organization. Successful leaders employ people with a diversity of experience and opinion, and support efforts to anticipate and embrace change, build productive work communities, and disperse leadership and responsibility.

The other volumes in this series are *On Mission and Leadership*, which explores the essential role that mission plays in defining and supporting leadership; *On Leading Change*, which explores the challenges of bringing organizations through transformation; and *On Creativity, Innovation, and Renewal*, which explores how leaders can keep an organization changing with a focus on building the future.

We gathered the wisdom of our contributors so that our readers could find insight and inspiration to make a difference in their organizations and their communities. We hope our collection will help you to lead, to inspire a change, to strengthen your performance, or to spark and sustain a renewal. We wish you the best as you apply these lessons to the work you do and the people you touch.

February 2002

Frances Hesselbein
Easton, Pennsylvania

Rob Johnston
New York, New York

About the Editors

Frances Hesselbein is chairman of the board of governors of the Peter F. Drucker Foundation for Nonprofit Management and is the former chief executive of the Girl Scouts of the U.S.A. She is a member of the boards of other organizations and corporations and is the lead editor of the Drucker Foundation's best-selling books, including *The Leader of the Future*, *The Organization of the Future*, *The Community of the Future*, *Leading Beyond the Walls*, and *Leader to Leader*, published by Jossey-Bass. She also serves as editor in chief of the journal *Leader to Leader*. She speaks on leadership and management to audiences around the world in the private, nonprofit, and governmental sectors. She has received fifteen honorary doctorates and was awarded the Presidential Medal of Freedom in 1998.

Rob Johnston is president and CEO of the Peter F. Drucker Foundation for Nonprofit Management. He has served the Drucker Foundation since 1991 and was appointed president effective March 2001. At the foundation he has led program development, the Drucker Innovation Award program, publication development, and teleconference and conference development.

He was executive producer for *Leading in a Time of Change*, a 2001 video featuring Peter F. Drucker and Peter M. Senge, and for *The Nonprofit Leader of the Future*, the foundation's 1997 video teleconference broadcast to 10,000 leaders across the United States. He leads the editorial development of the foundation's Web site (drucker.org) and is a senior editor for *Leader to Leader*. Johnston earned a B.A. degree in the history of art from Yale and an M.B.A. degree from Stanford. He contributed a chapter to *Enterprising Nonprofits* (John Wiley & Sons, 2001).

1

Putting One's House in Order

Frances Hesselbein

*The first step to "put one's house in order" is to employ
Peter Drucker's concept of "planned abandonment" and to
reject outmoded organizational policies, practices, and products. This involves reviewing the organization's mission,
customers, what the customers value, results, and plans to
attain organizational goals. A second step is to examine the
organization's leadership strengths, needs, and approaches;
its allocation and development of human resources; its communication of mission and values; and its diversity. The
third step of proactive change is introspection and planning
for personal development. By aligning the organization's
plan for the future with its plan for leadership and our own
personal plans, we become more integrated and innovative.*

Jack Welch, former chairman and CEO of General Electric,
once compared his organization to an old house. Over many
years all organizations, especially established ones, accumulate
outmoded practices, policies, and procedures; the leader's job, he
said, is to clean out the attics and closets. We need to take stock,
assess our organizational estate, and discard what no longer works.
Clearing the cobwebs from this old house is an adventure in
"planned abandonment," to use Peter Drucker's evocative phrase.

1

As this year fades, it is natural to look back to what we have accomplished and look ahead to what is possible. It is a time of profound assessment. We know that the future demands a new approach to planning, and to leading change. "Business as usual" is dead. Vision, mission, and courage will carry the day.

To move from vision to action, to lead vibrant organizations that can flourish in the 2000s, consider an exercise that for generations has helped people refresh and renew their lives: spring house cleaning. A passionate western Pennsylvania value (my roots are showing), this practice is invaluable in the life of an organization and its leaders.

Three Dimensions of Change

For today's organizations, cleaning the attic—"getting one's house in order"—means, first of all, revisiting one's *mission:* the short, powerful, compelling statement of why the organization does what it does, its reason for being. From a passionate, relevant mission flow the few powerful goals that reflect the organization's vision of the future. And from those goals flow the objectives, action steps, and organizational tactics that will carry the enterprise forward. We ask the five classic questions that Peter Drucker has charged organizations to answer for the past 60 years: What is our mission? Who is the customer? What does the customer value? What are our results? What is our plan?

But creating this organizational coherence is just the first imperative of change. The second dimension of good housekeeping is the plan for the *leadership* of the organization. Preparing our leadership house for the future requires as much time, energy, and rigor as the strategic plan for the enterprise itself.

To create a plan for the leadership corps we must ask ourselves several more questions. These include:

What are our leadership strengths?

What are the areas to be strengthened?

Are we leading from the front? Do we anticipate change and articulate shared aspirations, or simply react to crises?

How do we deploy our leaders, our teams, our people to further the mission and achieve our goals?

Do we use job expansion, job rotation, and opportunities for development in innovative ways to release the energies of people and increase job satisfaction?

Do our leaders see themselves as the embodiment of the mission, values, and beliefs of the organization?

How can we sharpen communication skills and attitudes—knowing communication is not merely saying something, it is being heard?

Are we building today the richly diverse, inclusive, cohesive organization that our vision and mission demand?

The answers to these questions help us build effective teams, deploy appropriate resources, and develop energetic leaders in response to goals and objectives.

The third dimension of change—getting our *personal* house in order—is perhaps the most challenging, and most neglected. It requires reserving the time, building the psychic energy, for introspection. When society is transformed, the organization is transformed, and in the end, we ourselves are transformed. We play an active role in all three.

Just as leaders are responsible for understanding their organization's strengths and preparing for its future, we must assess our personal strengths and take responsibility for planning our own development. For each of us, this will require listening to the whispers of our lives. We look at the intensely personal challenges of our health, our well-being, our relationships with others, and the promptings of our spiritual life—however we define it.

Bringing the Search Home

From such reflection we can set the goals of our own work—for instance, work-life balance—and ensure that our lives are consistent with the values and mission of the organization we are building. In our personal plan—written, not rolling around in our head—we are responsible for our own development, with checkpoints along the way.

I once talked with a highly successful CEO who shared with me his plan for 2000—he called it his "learning journey." It included fewer "things to do," greater focus, and more time for writing and for family—and specified deadlines for action. This went far beyond the business plan for a successful organization; it was the personal plan for a successful life.

When we align the organization's plan for the future with the plan for its leadership and with our own personal plan, they become one: the powerful symbol of the integrated, innovative organization of the future and its leaders. We look to other leaders, past or present, whose personal vision and values were congruent with the credo, the values of their organization. For instance, James Burke, former CEO of Johnson & Johnson, continues to inspire and motivate through his example, his results, his legacy.

Effective leaders have learned that moving from vision to reality requires a road map, a business plan for the future. When we create a vision for the institution, its leadership, and ourselves, we create a new house. We have left behind business as usual in all we see and do. It is an exuberant journey. It is called managing the dream.

Frances Hesselbein is editor in chief of *Leader to Leader*, chairman of the board of governors of the Drucker Foundation, and former chief executive of the Girl Scouts of the U.S.A.

2

High Reliability

The Power of Mindfulness

Karl Weick and Kathleen Sutcliffe, with David Obstfeld

The effectiveness of high-reliability organizations, such as air traffic control centers, stems from the ability to respond to fluctuating conditions. Collective mindfulness, which can be developed in any organization, consists of: (1) viewing any failure as a systemic problem to be examined and learned from; (2) reluctance to simplify interpretations; (3) integrated sensitivity to and communication about operations throughout the organization; (4) commitment to resilience; and (5) fluidity of decision-making structures.

A patient is wheeled into the emergency room in cardiac arrest. A team of doctors and nurses leaps into action. Within minutes the patient's heart rate is stabilized and the team disperses.

The crew of an aircraft carrier works nonstop, managing the steady stream of take-offs and landings. In a moment of crisis crew members with appropriate experience break ranks, quickly form a group to contain the crisis, then return to their positions.

In a quiet air traffic control center, several controllers leave their posts to assist a colleague managing an unusually high volume of traffic. Backup controllers step into the vacated positions. Gradually people fall back to their original stations.

Casual observers might think these were tightly scripted, well-rehearsed activities. Individual players knew their roles, had often encountered these situations, and had only to do what they had always done to work effectively and reliably. However, research on operations such as these—known as high-reliability organizations (HROs) because of the potential for catastrophic outcomes should they fail to execute—reveals that the opposite is true. Their reliability is not due solely to standardized routines, which would have the individuals enacting the same set of actions over and over. Rather, their reliability comes from an ability to ensure stable outcomes despite working conditions—and responses to those conditions—that can vary wildly.

What do HROs have to do with other organizations? After all, unlike a nuclear power plant, neonatal care unit, or warship, most enterprises operate in a relatively forgiving environment. However, with increased competition, high customer expectations, and reduced cycle time, today's business environment is in fact very harsh. Although lives may not be at stake, livelihoods may be. All high-performance organizations aim to deliver the consistency, quality, and responsiveness of the best HROs. Yet as they are driven to squeeze slack out of their operations through downsizing, mergers, resource reduction, or complex distributed computer technologies, these same organizations are at risk for a host of failures.

Furthermore, most enterprises look for ways to give individuals the opportunity to build expertise, discover and correct errors, and apply their learning to each new problem—what HROs do at their best. We call this organizational competence *collective mindfulness*. By that we mean the capacity of groups and individuals to be acutely aware of significant details, to notice errors in the making, and to have the shared expertise and freedom to act on what they notice. Like other organizational capabilities, mindfulness can be developed through effective organizational and leadership practices.

Five Keys to Mindfulness

In reviewing years of research on HROs, we looked for how these organizations sustain reliability in the face of persistent high risks and fluctuating conditions. What operational or organizational strategies allow them to respond effectively to sudden changes? We discovered that a state of collective mindfulness grows out of five qualities common to the best HROs:

- Preoccupation with failure
- Reluctance to simplify interpretations
- Sensitivity to operations
- Commitment to resilience
- Fluidity of decision-making structures

Each of these qualities encompasses a distinctive set of organizational skills.

Preoccupation with Failure

It is through failure—trial and error—that much learning in organizations occurs. But because the cost of failure is so high, and the occurrence of any given type of failure so rare, HROs have fewer opportunities for such learning. Therefore, they must find ways to do more with less information, to maximize what they can learn from the failures that do occur.

Effective HROs encourage the reporting of errors and regard any failure, no matter how seemingly isolated, as a signal of possible weakness elsewhere. This is a very different approach from that of most organizations, which tend to localize failures and view them as specific rather than systemic problems. Many researchers have observed a by-product of this attentiveness to all failures. In contrast to their minor role in most organizations, maintenance departments in HROs become central locations for organizational learning. Maintenance workers tend to encounter the largest number of failures, at earlier stages of development, and have an ongoing sense of vulnerabilities in technology, sloppiness in operations, gaps in procedures, and sequences by which one error triggers another.

To further increase their knowledge base, the best HROs also encourage and reward the reporting of errors, even going so far as to reward those who have committed them. Researchers Martin Landau and Donald Chisholm, for example, describe a seaman on the nuclear carrier *Carl Vinson* who reported the loss of a tool on the deck. All aircraft aloft were redirected to land bases until the tool was found, and the seaman was commended for his action—recognizing a potential danger—the next day at a formal ceremony. Similarly, Harvard Business School professor Amy Edmondson found, contrary to her hypotheses, that the best-performing nursing units had *higher* detected rates for adverse drug events than did lower-performing units. She interprets these results to mean not that more errors were committed in the better units, but that a climate of openness made people more willing to report and discuss errors and to work toward correcting them.

What also sets effective HROs apart is the way they perceive failure in relation to success. The best HROs regard close calls—for example, a near collision in aviation—as a kind of failure that reveals potential danger. Less effective HROs see close calls as evidence of success and an ability to avoid disaster.

Reluctance to Simplify Interpretations

Humans handle complex tasks by simplifying their interpretation of events. These simplified worldviews, frameworks, or mind-sets allow people to ignore information that may hamper efficient decision making. Indeed, all organizations are defined by what they ignore. This means, of course, that they are also defined by what can surprise them. Effective HROs pay attention to what is overlooked in the effort to manage ambiguity; they generally know more about what they *don't* know. Some have characterized this as an attempt to match external complexity with internal complexity. This effort takes a variety of forms, such as checks and balances embedded in diverse committees and meetings, frequent adversarial reviews, recruitment of employees who bring new experience and expertise, frequent job rotation, and retraining.

HROs continuously assess their procedures, rejecting some and adjusting others, to fight complacency and rigidity. This ongoing process of renewal and reevaluation requires a diverse set of perspectives within the organization, as well as mechanisms that allow those perspectives to be applied. This is not a simple matter.

A group with many diverse perceptions has more information at its disposal; what it may not have is a way of tapping the full range of this information. As diverse groups work to solve

problems—whether to contain an emerging crisis or to formu-
late long-term strategy—they run the danger of drawing on only
those perceptions that are held in common, while ignoring, dis-
carding, or discounting perceptions that are unique. Because it
is typically the perceptions that are *not* common, the ones that
diverge from the norm, that hold the key to detection of dangerous anomalies, HROs put a premium on skills that allow
groups to uncover unique information. For this reason, effective
HROs tend to nurture interpersonal skills, mutual respect, and
trust, and discourage hubris, stubbornness, and self-importance.

These attributes also allow HROs to cultivate a high degree
of skepticism with the aim of combating the human tendency
to simplify. When a report is met with skepticism and the skep-
tic makes an independent assessment, there are then two observations where originally there had been only one. The second
set of observations may itself be double-checked by still another.
This redundancy is based on the notion that all humans are fal-
lible and that skeptics improve reliability.

Sensitivity to Operations

People in effective HROs tend to pay close attention to operations, and they consider such attentiveness an enterprisewide
task. Even the most talented and sophisticated leaders have a
limited ability to register the entirety of an organization and its
complex operating environment. HRO leaders, therefore, deploy resources so that many others can see what is happening,
comprehend what it means, and project into the near future
what these understandings predict will happen. By developing
an integrated picture of operations in the moment, people make
many small adjustments that prevent errors from accumulating.

Maintaining a heightened awareness of current operations must be a shared responsibility, one that is in a constant state of revision. How do HROs achieve this sensitivity to operations? In nuclear power plants, for example, the key to a successful "planned outage"—a difficult maintenance procedure—is not only the formal delegation of authority to craft workers but also the nearly complete availability of top management to provide support. This assures that any problem can rapidly receive the attention it requires at all levels of the organization, according to Mathilde Bourrier, in research for the European research consortium COTCOS.

This approach captures what occurs in effective HROs as they employ a range of strategies—such as situation assessments with continual updates and active diagnosis of planned procedures—to sustain a collective sensitivity to all aspects of operations. What emerges is a rich picture of ongoing group interaction and communication about actual operations and workplace characteristics. Because this complex level of awareness is beyond any single individual, effective HROs tend to be more aware of the potential for overload of any one of their members.

Commitment to Resilience

Anticipation, in the words of the late political scientist Aaron Wildavsky, involves the "prediction and prevention of potential dangers before damage is done." He defined resilience, on the other hand, as "the capacity to cope with unanticipated dangers after they have become manifest, learning to bounce back." Traditional organizations typically rely on anticipation of expected surprises, risk aversion, and planned defenses against foreseeable risks. Effective HROs, however, are both anticipatory *and* resilient. The capacity for resilience is what sets HROs apart from traditional organizations, and manifests itself in many forms.

The aircraft carrier crews who organize into ad hoc teams, provide expert problem solving, and return to other duties when a crisis abates exemplify resilience. Such teams allow for rapid pooling of expertise to handle events that are impossible to anticipate. The ability to come together informally as the situation demands increases the knowledge and actions that can be brought to bear on a problem. However, resilience involves more than simply knowing how to regroup during a crisis and keep going. To be resilient also means being able to come away from the event with an even greater capacity to prevent and contain future errors.

Another critical element of resilience is the capacity for improvisation, which allows the organization to expand exponentially not only the range of actions in its repertoire but also the range of potential threats it can foresee. People tend to notice what they can do something about; the greater their capacity to improvise, the greater the variety of threats they are able to anticipate. Ultimately, resilience brings an improved ability both to anticipate and to deal with the unanticipated. For example, medication errors in an intensive care unit were reduced about 66 percent when a pharmacist was added to a team of doctors and nurses making rounds. By expanding the network and range of capabilities, the team was able to notice more mistakes and correct them before they became catastrophic.

Fluidity of Decision-Making Structures

One obvious strategy for reducing error would seem to be the adoption of orderly procedures. Yet even though specified procedures have a place in HROs, they can also backfire by expanding the effects of errors that do occur. For example, an investigation of the space shuttle *Challenger* disaster showed that NASA's orderly routines enabled the erosion of O-rings to persist and be accepted as normal by more units than if procedures had been less regimented. Any orderly hierarchy can amplify errors, especially when those miscues occur near the top. Higher-level errors tend to fuel lower-level errors, making the results harder to manage. As seen in the *Challenger* incident, it is the very reliability that HROs cultivate that makes it possible for small errors to spread, accumulate, interact, and trigger serious consequences. Ironically, HROs are sometimes failure-free in spite of their orderliness, not because of it.

To guard against these dangers (and to enhance the capacity for resilience), effective HROs allow for moments of organized anarchy. Whereas in a closed hierarchical structure, critical choices are made by "important"—high-ranking—decision makers, the best HROs loosen the designation of who is important when certain problems arise. This allows decision making to migrate to people who may have more relevant expertise—and increases the likelihood that new capabilities will be matched with new problems. Migration achieves flexibility as well as orderliness. These HROs recognize—and operationalize—a principle that often escapes decision makers at critical moments: expertise and experience are usually more important than rank. HROs allow expertise at the bottom of the pyramid to rise to the top when needed.

For example, Loma Linda Children's Hospital has developed a way to prevent the accidental displacement of a patient's throat tube. When a nurse believes that the child's agitation may cause the tube to be dislodged, the nurse asks the resident physician for an order to increase sedation or paralysis. Residents have been taught to respect the nurses' recommendations. Requests by the nurse for an increase in medication are not denied.

Lessons from HROs

Effective HROs present a compelling picture of people working in fluid but orderly ways to focus energy and expertise where and when they are needed. The best HROs understand the dangers of complacency, inattention, and predictable routines, all of which can increase the likelihood of error. They maintain a delicate and complex balance of processes that encourage continuous learning and improvement, while at the same time promoting order and reliable performance. This is a powerful combination.

What are some of the specific lessons that other organizations can learn from HROs? How can others develop the five qualities that drive HROs toward mindful action? To enhance collective mindfulness, leaders must

- *Cultivate humility.* Appreciate the traps inherent in short-term success and false optimism. Leaders try to see the value of increasing organizational learning through a healthy skepticism about their own accomplishments and a greater awareness of potentials for failure.

- *Seek variety.* Reassess networks within one's system with an eye for the diversity of experience, expertise, and perspective they bring together to solve problems. Then create processes, practices, and interpersonal skills to resolve the conflicts that can result from such diversity.

- *Invent new models.* Consider how to loosen hierarchies so that the number of ad hoc networks of expertise can be expanded. Use frontline people— for example, those who work with warranty returns, customer service, or tech support hot lines—as key troubleshooters, much like the maintenance workers in HROs.

- *Be flexible.* Look for ways to foster true resilience to offset lapses in anticipation and forecasting. As pressures increase to do more with less, develop strategies for guarding against job burnout.

- *Build excess capacity.* Realize that by eliminating apparently redundant positions one may be losing experience and expertise, and that loss can limit the repertoire of responses available to the organization.

- *Question assumptions.* Understand that leadership is as much about managing error as it is about achieving formal organizational goals—and explore how people in the organization decide what constitutes error and how they preserve attention to reliability.

In the face of increasingly complex and competing demands, all enterprises—in manufacturing, education, finance, public service—operate in a less and less forgiving environment. Pressures for reliability are increasing for all organizations (as evidenced, for instance, in the total quality movement of recent years). When Saturn has to inform customers that their car seats are defective and need to be replaced, when tainted cans of Coca-Cola are found in Belgium, or when airlines regularly lose passengers' luggage, the effects may not be catastrophic (no one may die), but the losses these companies suffer—measured in customer confidence and resources spent to rectify the errors—can be huge. In the face of massive consequences from unforeseen events, mindfulness is a skill that no organization can afford to ignore.

Karl Weick is the Rensis Likert Collegiate Professor of Organizational Behavior and Psychology, and professor of psychology, at the University of Michigan Business School. His books include the influential *Sensemaking in Organizations* and *The Social Psychology of Organizing*, named by *Inc. Magazine* as one of the nine best business books ever written. His research focuses on management of uncertainty under pressure.

Kathleen Sutcliffe is associate professor of organizational behavior and human resource management at the University of Michigan Business School. She has previously worked as a program consultant to the state of Alaska and a senior manager for a large health care organization. She has consulted to high-tech companies, major retailers, and public agencies. Her research focuses on organizational resilience and adaptability.

David Obstfeld is the former director of training and development at Fannie Mae. He has conducted research in automotive, chemical, pharmaceutical, and financial service industries, focusing on the social processes of innovation, and has a Ph.d. in business administration from the University of Michigan.

3

The Marketing
of Leadership

Philip Kotler

*Leaders must be able to market their visions and organiza-
tions to employees, customers, suppliers, partners, and investors. This starts with identifying stakeholders' needs and
expectations. Internal marketing is accomplished through getting into the trenches, listening and responding to employees,
using 360-degree feedback to assess leader performance, articulating a worthy goal and how people's work contributes to
the goal, providing growth opportunities and a positive work
environment, and providing financial and psychic rewards.*

It has often been noted that we need to develop strong leaders at every level of the organization. We count on people
throughout our workplaces and communities to provide the vision, context, understanding, and resources for the future. We
also need leaders who understand marketing. Marketing is not
just the job of the marketing department. It is a key skill needed
by leaders.

Leaders who hope to make a difference must be able to market their visions and ideas to many groups within and outside
the organization. Today's CEO needs to take a *stakeholder view*,
not only a *shareholder view*, of the enterprise. History suggests

that the approach exemplified by former Scott Paper and Sunbeam CEO Al Dunlap—ruthlessly cutting costs, eliminating jobs, and shortchanging supplier and distributor relations in order to increase short-run profits (and temporarily inflate stock prices)—has been taken as far as it can go. There is little fat to spare in most organizations today, and the marginal gains that can be realized from that approach too often put the future of the enterprise in jeopardy.

An effective leader knows that the organization is only as strong as its weakest link. Unhappy employees, suppliers, distributors, dealers, or end-users can sink the ship. An increasing number of CEOs are managing their companies—Hewlett-Packard, Xerox, Rockwell, and many others—with "the Balanced Scorecard" approach developed by Robert Kaplan of Harvard, which measures customer and employee satisfaction, innovation, knowledge creation, and effectiveness of mission as well as financial performance.

The widespread downsizing in recent times has almost fatally hurt employee loyalty. In far too many companies, employees simply don't trust their bosses. That mistrust, as executives and shareholders are learning, carries a high price. Employees are increasingly looking out for themselves. Especially in knowledge-based organizations, they are taking the "new employment contract" at face value, cultivating valuable skills that in today's tight labor market they can sell to the highest bidder. It is a major challenge for a CEO to rebuild a culture of loyalty that has been destroyed by downsizing. Unless the bosses also take pay cuts when they impose one on the troops and otherwise commit themselves to the kind of teamwork and new ways of working that they demand of their constituents, they simply won't be trusted. In the absence of that trust, no meaningful change can be sustained.

Knowing the Internal Market

Hal Rosenbluth, who runs a national travel agency with $2.5 billion in revenue, wrote a best-selling book with the surprising title *The Customer Comes Second*. In service businesses such as hotels, restaurants, and banks, satisfying the employee is arguably the No. 1 job of managers. Bill Marriott Jr. says that if he has managed to satisfy his employees, then they will satisfy the customers, the customers will come back to Marriott hotels, and the stockholders will be rewarded. So Marriott and other service leaders work hard to meet the interests of their employees. This task has been called *internal marketing* because managers are trying to sense, serve, and satisfy an internal market, the employees.

Leaders can better learn the needs of their internal customers in a number of ways. General Electric's Jack Welch instituted the Work-Out program, in which his division heads listened to their employees' ideas, gripes, and suggestions and got back to them with answers. Many companies, including industry leaders like Levi Strauss, Sun Microsystems, Nortel, and GE, use 360-degree feedback for employees to assess their bosses' performance in key areas of leadership and management.

Increasingly, managers have a personal stake in employees' and customers' effectiveness. But bosses need not wait for formal feedback to identify their organization's and their personal strengths and weaknesses. They can understand their workers' needs by getting into the trenches and assuming a worker's role. For instance, one week a year senior managers at McDonald's, at Disney, and at ServiceMaster leave their offices and take up the job of cooking hamburgers, taking tickets, cleaning hospital rooms, and meeting employees and customers. Such frontline exposure gives executives important insights into the internal and external market and sends a message to employees that management is concerned about the real-world issues of serving customers.

Selling the Dream

What distinguishes leaders from managers is the ability to articulate not just a working plan but an inspiring dream. Both are essential, but leaders have a more challenging responsibility than managers. They must stretch the sights of their followers to embrace a worthy goal to be reached, and show how people's everyday work contributes to the goal. And that goal must be articulated not in financial terms so much as in social-benefit terms. A fertilizer company does not simply make fertilizer; its aspiration should be to help feed the hungry. A hotel does not simply peddle rooms; it creates a home away from home. Combined with effective internal marketing of the company's professional growth opportunities, positive work environment, and financial and psychic rewards, a clear and compelling mission provides powerful incentives for employees to commit their best efforts. Consider the simplicity—and hence the power—of Microsoft's mission: "to put a computer on every desktop and in every home." Or Avon Products: "to understand and satisfy the product, service, and self-fulfillment needs of women globally." Or Coca-Cola: "to place a Coke within an arm's reach everywhere in the world."

Leaders, in short, communicate the unique mission, vision, and values of the organization to customers, employees, investors or donors, and communities. They are strategists, ambassadors, and evangelists for their organization and its cause. They are, in the fullest sense of the word, marketers. Effective marketing, after all, begins with a deep understanding of and respect for the customer—and senior executives serve many customers inside and outside the walls of the organization. In a truly customer-focused organization, leaders, like marketers, communicate that understanding and respect through the quality of their daily actions.

Looking from the Outside In

It's easy for those in such disciplines as manufacturing, finance, or operations to focus on the inner workings of the organization and miss seeing when the company is out of sync with the changing marketplace. CEOs with a marketing background more readily recognize the rapidly changing currents in the marketplace and can sense when new initiatives are needed to keep the ship afloat. They take the broadest possible view of marketing, looking beyond promotion and distribution, or even market research and strategy. They see marketing as an enterprisewide philosophy of value and wealth creation, as Peter Drucker so keenly expressed.

Effective leaders, like effective marketers, are outside-in thinkers, not inside-out thinkers. They start with the needs of the marketplace, not with the needs of the organization. Great products and services are designed in the marketplace—literally—with customers taking the lead in expressing their needs and assisting companies in developing solutions.

That is why a major task of the leader is to get everyone in the organization to see the customer as the center of their universe. Staff members must recognize that the company doesn't pay them; the customers do. Senior management must spell out how each group and individual in the company affects customer satisfaction and retention, and what it costs the company when a customer is lost. They must remind people throughout the organization that the essence of marketing is not selling, nor even the "four P's" of product, price, place, and promotion. The essence of marketing is the voluntary and beneficial *exchange of value*. Whether the "buyer" be a customer, employee, investor, or funder, both parties in any transaction must feel they are gaining more than they are giving up. Unless the organization understands that buyer well enough to offer clear perceived value, there is no basis for an exchange.

New Models of Marketing

Unfortunately for most organizations, that broad understanding of customers, and of marketing itself, is unusual. Too many companies are still product-centered and product-organized. They want their marketers to sell their products, whether or not those products match what customers at the time really need and want. And that is why CEOs increasingly express their disappointment with the performance of their marketing operations. Each year they budget more money for marketing—the lion's share of which typically goes to advertising, sales promotion, and sales activity—and seem to get less for it. These companies are still practicing mass marketing and failing to recognize the highly varying needs of groups and individuals within the market. In recent years, fortunately, some companies are scaling their marketing programs to more clearly targeted groups and individuals and are achieving more measurable results.

The CEO must play a major role in installing a newer type of marketing in the organization, one using the new tools and technologies available for marketing in the new millennium. The CEO should be the organization's chief marketing officer. As such, he or she should participate personally in some marketing engagements, especially selling large business-to-business projects. CEOs of companies that buy large information systems, power systems, and other critical items are usually involved in the purchase decision. It makes sense for the CEO of the selling company to be equally involved.

Part of Lou Gerstner's success in revitalizing IBM is the result of his spending 30 percent of his time meeting customers. GE's Jack Welch also recognized the importance of selling from the top. He changed the title of each major division chief from vice president to CEO; GE now has 13 CEOs to call on senior executives in customer companies. Welch personally called on over 100 of GE's major customers each year. Equally important, he devoted at least half his time to his company's "people issues," visiting with, assessing, and cultivating management talent, and leading monthly sessions at GE's Crotonville training center. He engaged thousands of managers in the course of his work, articulated company goals and expectations, and made clear that it is part of the manager's job to identify and exploit market opportunities. As GE's performance demonstrates, that approach is not only great leadership, it is great marketing.

How Leaders Use Marketing Skills

Just as good leadership practices—defining a vision, building shared values, looking beyond the boundaries of the organization—can enhance marketing, so too can the principles of effective marketing enhance leadership. Like good marketers, leaders must understand the needs and expectations of their audience—and understand their own strengths and weaknesses. Rather than trying to be all things to all people, they must know who they are and be true both to themselves and to their vision

e. They may be gazelles, moving quickly to correct
but they cannot be chameleons, changing colors to
the circumstances.

Leaders must deliver on their promises. That is the leadership equivalent of the money-back guarantee. Every great brand
builds trust, confidence, and rapport with those who use that
product. So too must leaders be reliable and keep faith with customers, employees, and investors.

That a customer-focused, mission-based mind-set is essential
to both marketing strategy and effective leadership is evident in
the rise of broader marketing applications—the marketing of social ideas, places, and organizations. Whether advancing a cause,
an entire community, or an institution, leaders are usually trying to influence behavior; they are asking others to take action,
to donate time or money, or to make a commitment in return
for achieving a desired change. They must not just provide a way
to contribute but be able to show that each contribution is ap-
preciated and has made a difference.

Effective nonprofit leaders understand that the services they
provide are largely inseparable from the people who deliver
those services or from the organization as a whole. They are
therefore tireless in

- Reminding volunteers and staff of the organization's
  reason for being
- Establishing a customer-first attitude at the front line
- Providing feedback systems and measuring results
- Giving people the tools to make decisions and act in
  the best interests of the customers

- Matching responsibilities to individual capabilities,
setting clear goals, and treating volunteers and staff
like the professionals they are

Such practices, well understood in the nonprofit world, are
having an impact on businesses as well. They are the essence
not only of good leadership practices but of good marketing.

Reading the Future

Yet another marketing skill that serves leaders well is antici-
pating the future. Smart marketers—and effective leaders—try
to imagine both new threats and new opportunities. In fact,
they are able to tease out opportunities that might initially appear to be threats. It doesn't take much sleuthing to see what is
happening around us.

- The dramatic aging of industrial societies and the
growing need for health care, financial services,
alternative housing arrangements, and other personal services. Remember, though, our older population will be very different in nature, not just in size,
from past generations. The attitudes of those now
55 and older remain closer to those of 35- to 40-
year-olds than their parents' were at a similar age;
in old age as in youth, Baby Boomers will be unlike
any cohort that preceded them.

- The growing segmentation of the population into
high- and low-income groups, with the once rock-
solid middle class shrinking. Increasingly, companies

will have to target their offerings either to affluent consumers demanding top quality and personalized service or to those demanding no-frills products and services at the lowest possible price.

- Consumers' demand for entertainment and its influence on travel, retailing, even museums, schools, and libraries, which now try to create an "experience" that attracts new customers. Organizations must learn to provide a destination or an event, not just a place of business or a service.

- All customers' rising expectations for quality, pricing, and service excellence. Even at the low end of the market, consumers expect basic levels of quality, service, or convenience. The key is to design every product or service to meet the price and quality demands of a specific target group.

These trends have clear implications for marketers, but also for organizational leaders who must develop strategies that suit the changing needs of the workforce as well as those of the marketplace.

Organizing for Success

Whether we realize the full potential of our organizations' marketing capability will depend largely on another question that only senior leaders can decide—how the organization, and the marketing function itself, is structured. To reduce turf battles and improve responsiveness, many organizations' sales, marketing, R&D, distribution, and finance departments are becoming far more integrated. This does not mean that the marketing department should be dismantled; market planning, strategy, and coordination are key activities that logically belong to a marketing unit. But as in all realms of the new organization, marketers' responsibilities and relationships are changing. Thus the power of once-omnipotent brand managers, who controlled the destiny of their particular product, might be supplanted by market managers, who see what strategies or product mix will best serve the needs of each particular market group; or by process managers, who integrate the diverse activities involved in achieving a particular set of customer-based outcomes.

That is why leaders can never be far removed from the marketing function. A key role of leadership—focusing people's attention on what is best for the customer and for the organization, rather than for any one department—becomes paramount. As Hewlett-Packard cofounder David Packard has said, "Marketing is far too important to leave to the marketing department." In the end, marketing, which by definition must focus on the market, is the CEO's—and everyone's—business.

Philip Kotler is the S.C. Johnson & Son Distinguished Professor of International Marketing at the J.L. Kellogg Graduate School of Management, Northwestern University. He has written more than 100 articles for leading business journals and is author or coauthor of 22 books, translated into 20 languages. These include *Marketing Management, Principles of Marketing,* and *Social Marketing.*

4

The View from a Cubicle

An Interview with Scott Adams

The creator of the widely read Dilbert *comic strip notes the
need for honest communication throughout an organization;
the need for people to believe that there is some reason for
their work; the need to contribute to people's productivity
rather than get in the way of it; the need for opening a channel to the customer; the need for "enlightened capitalism";
and the benefits of shared experience and flexible, varying
work teams. He espouses the idea of generating performance
contracts so that the boss is the worker's customer. He also
discusses the pitfalls of cubicles, performance measurement,
employee recognition, phony team exercises, and other frustrating issues.*

One of the most influential management observers of the
1990s works from a simple home office in Danville, California. He spent nine years working in a cubicle office at Pacific
Bell. But Scott Adams reaches 1.5 million people every day, and
his *Dilbert* comic strip, books, and TV show shine a harsh, silly,
and often deadly accurate light on today's workplace. As the
New York Times noted, he "clearly knows . . . about the wrong
way to run a business." He spoke with Paul Cohen and Alan

Shrader about his views of management, management gurus, and his own work practices.

Leader to Leader: Scott, in a world full of management gurus, you may be the first antimanagement guru. Do you see yourself as kind of an antidote to gurus? Should young people read your work as an inoculation against all that they will encounter in the workplace?

Scott Adams: I never think of myself as against gurus. The thing I'm shooting for is a point of view. I'm giving you the employee-in-the-cubicle point of view. That's very distinct from what a lot of consultants and gurus do. Usually they drop in by parachute, talk to the executives, and go away having no idea what the employees are thinking. Sometimes it doesn't matter. Sometimes you're shoving something down people's throats and all you want is higher stock price. Getting touchy-feely with employees may be counterproductive to your mission.

I'm not trying to present solutions. But to the extent that it's useful to show what things are silly or objectionable or just annoying from the employee's point of view, that can translate to some benefits if somebody chooses to use it that way. It would be interesting to have a new employee handbook that was just Dilbert cartoons; that would certainly tell you what you were getting into—but it's not my goal.

L2L: It seems that at least one speaker at every management conference uses a Dilbert cartoon to illustrate a point. So senior managers, not only cubicle workers, seem to appreciate your point of view. If that's the case, why does the absurdity persist?

SA: Often absurdity is more desirable than the alternative. I'll give you an example. A high-level manager in a large organization who was considering implementing casual Friday asked for my opinion. I explained that there's nothing funnier than the notion that it would be safe to allow people to dress comfortably one day of the week but that if you extended it to two, perhaps that would hurt your stock price or morale. But, having said that, I went on to support the notion of casual Friday because it's 20 percent better than not having it at all. So here you have a clear example of absurdity—one day that casual is OK—being better than the nonabsurd alternative, all casual or all noncasual. So absurdity is often the comfortable compromise. That is just an oddity of the world.

L2L: What is the most absurd practice that you've seen in businesses?

SA: There are few things that top cubicles. If you know the history of the cubicle—the original idea, just over 30 years ago, was that everyone has different requirements for desk space and storage space. So if you built an environment that was modular, then everyone could pick and choose the components that were appropriate for their function. But when big companies saw it, they said, "You know, if we made them all exactly the same, these should be really cheap." So the myth put forward is that this will help communication and allow the free flow of knowledge, when in fact it's just cheaper. Nobody's fooled by the myth. But telling people, "We're saving a lot of money, so just get in your little box," wouldn't work. Again, it's more comfortable to compromise on the absurd.

L2L: Others call it living with paradox.

SA: Yes. The Dilbert Principle, in my book of the same name, is another example: "The most ineffective workers are systematically moved to the place where they can do the least damage—management." That wasn't just a comic exaggeration; I was actually observing that the least skilled people were being promoted specifically so that you didn't waste your skilled people in those jobs. And nothing could be more absurd than putting the least competent people in a job that has leverage on everybody's results.

L2L: You treat bosses harshly in your work. Is there something about being in a position of authority in an organization that brings out the worst in people?

SA: In Dilbert's world, the technical world, where Dilbert is an MIT graduate with double 800s on the SATs, there are things that he sees as obvious that his boss is not going to see. But it has always amused me that you can go anywhere and the guy in the John Deere hat will get off the tractor and tell you why NAFTA won't work and why trade policy needs to be different. And he won't say, "It's bad for me personally." He'll give you supply side economics and political theory. Everyone believes that they're smarter than the people in charge. But usually that's because they have less information. Every decision the boss makes may not appear to make perfect sense. But isn't it possible he knows something we don't?

L2L: But isn't that also a convenient dodge? "If you only knew what I knew." Or, "You don't have the whole picture."

SA: But then bosses can't say that because they'll be picked to death: "Are you saying there's going to be a reorganization? Is there a merger? I better stop working." Nothing is more damaging than the usual "what have you heard" rumor mongering. That's the kiss of death for productivity.

L2L: Did you ever have a good boss? And if so, what did that person do?

SA: People are surprised to hear that I had more good bosses than not. And the Dilbert world is every bad experience that I ever had with maybe 30 different bosses, plus experiences collected from others. For example, the boss who said, "My job is to give you what you need to do your job." We'd say, "We really need to create a budget. Can we talk to you next week?" And he'd be out for the next month, literally. He was completely unavailable to do the thing which he was just telling us was his only job. Otherwise, he was a great guy and smart and had lots of good things going for him.

L2L: Have you ever had to manage others? And if so, what did you learn from that?

SA: I was a bank supervisor and although I did not have my own office then, I had a taller cubicle. That's what you got. It was very special. I had—at the peak—nine people working for me. And they of course all had completely different requirements. I tried to treat them differently. My Rule Number 1 for bossdom is that you have to craft it to the specific person in that specific job. But that means that basically you're doomed if you have a group of even three people. You will be inconsistent— treating some people harshly and others with encouragement. I try to avoid being in that position.

The other thing I learned is that during that time I actually thought I was a good manager. Everyone I meet thinks they are good managers, too. Almost never will you meet a manager who says, "You know, I have to admit, I really am terrible at managing. Everybody hates me and I'm incompetent." No one says it because I think people don't believe it. And over time, I've come to grips with the fact that I probably was a bad manager, or certainly bad in some ways that were completely invisible to me, just as everyone else's faults are invisible to them. Some of the magic of managing is to somehow not see how you're destroying people's productivity.

L2L: How does a manager get a sense of what's really going on in the organization or with customers?

SA: The way I've seen it done is with spies. And what that usually means is befriending specific employees in key places who are at lower levels. Their incentive is they want to suck up to somebody who is in power, and your incentive is you want somebody who will actually tell you what people are saying. Of course, all information is imperfect but the spy method is the only one I've seen that is reliable. Even now, with no employees, I get filtered information. Every problem that I've ever heard about—from licensing to anything else—somebody out there was willing to tell me anonymously by e-mail. It's a pretty wonderful system.

L2L: You have noted that it's very hard to assess performance in most organizations. How would you handle performance assessment?

SA: You want to avoid any situation in which your success depends on motivating someone who can't be measured. You can't win that game. But I find that when people have contracts, they perform, because they treat you like a customer. There's an immediate, specific reason that they want you to be delighted with their work. But as soon as people become an employee, they feel like they're a kid in the family and you can't really disown them that easily. There's a process and paperwork and you don't want to feel you made the wrong decision to hire them in the first place. You're stuck.

L2L: You're saying don't be a boss—be a customer.

SA: Yes. And ultimately, put yourself in a position where you can assess by outcomes. But don't try to put objective measures on something that can't be quantified. I always told my employees that performance reviews didn't matter too much and that what mattered is whether they were getting better and were learning stuff.

L2L: You've said that most employee recognition and motivation efforts are degrading—pointing out, for instance, that senior managers don't get employee recognition. How should you recognize and acknowledge effort?

SA: I'll speak only as an employee who has been on the receiving end. What has worked for me is that somebody let the people I worked with know that I did a good job. Pure ego gratification. But the employee of the week thing—there was a case recently where the employees were mad because the only person who ever got the employee of the week was the top performer. That seemed so unfair. So management actually caved and started giving it out on a "fairer" basis—*everybody* got to be employee of the week.

L2L: In your ideal company, described in *The Dilbert Principle*, managers try to keep employees happy, not humiliate them, allow them to be productive, and let them leave at 5:00. Why is that so difficult for organizations?

SA: It's difficult mostly because you don't get to choose your employees. Often, you're the manager who comes in and you inherit a group and they're already disgruntled. All positive models of work depend on having people who want to be there and feel there's some reason to be working. Part of the problem also is that so many people have jobs where what they produce is invisible: I drafted a contract today. I improved how my biggest customer thinks about us—which is real, but you just can't see it. So you look for the stuff you can see—how long people are in the office and what they're wearing. You default to that because it's visible.

L2L: Have you found any leadership training approaches that have value?

SA: The only things that I think work are where people are doing the actual job, where they get shared experience and enjoy some success as a team. But taking them out and making them hang from ropes and trees—I once experienced a trust exercise where my partner jumped out of the way and let me fall on my butt, because she thought that I looked too heavy. I'm 5'8", and she outweighed me.

I also was in a problem-solving exercise where you had to get from one place to another by putting planks from some tree stump–like things to other tree stump things and then collect all the planks and get all your people to the other side. And I had a boss who ignored what everyone was saying and insisted on doing it his own way. It ended with all of us on the other side and him on a plank out in the middle. It was everything I needed to know—everything discouraging about where I worked. It was the clearest signal that we were doomed as a group.

L2L: You suggest that, outside of sports, the notion of team-work is dangerous. How do you think people should organize complex work that requires multiple types of expertise?

SA: I'm learning how they do stuff in Hollywood. Everything there is a virtual business. If you shoot a pilot episode, everybody's a free agent. You find your director, your writers, you put the thing together, a few people look at it—and then it dies, usually. Nineteen out of 20 pilots are never shown. So you disband and then some other group collects. It's a different model from anything you see in corporate America. If you're making a toothpaste in corporate America and it's not exactly right the first time, you do your focus group—keep working on it. In Hollywood you throw it away, and all the people scatter instantly. And they don't ever work together again except in ones and twos.

L2L: In Dilbert's world, the marketing department is always the enemy. Why?

SA: Things happen based on how you're trained. Economics people can talk to engineering people because you're always looking for the cheapest, easiest, simplest, most elegant solution. You're looking at complexity and trying to simplify. Marketing people are trying to hide reality. They're trying to take, for example, long distance telephone service, which is exactly the same no matter who you buy it from, and convince people that one is better. All of your instincts as an engineer are to be logical and simple and reliable—and in marketing, everything is to take what is clear and make it unclear. So when you put engineers and marketing people in the same room, it just doesn't work.

L2L: How have you approached the marketing of your ideas and products?

SA: If you look at my cartoon work, what was missing was, I didn't know what people liked or didn't. So I put my e-mail address in the strip and did what any business person does—I opened a channel to the customer. A standard business practice, but it never had been done because artists don't use standard business practices. And it worked, because standard business practice is standard because it usually works, at least when it comes to stuff like listening to the customer. The other thing that I'm a maniac about is to limit what I'm involved with—whether it's the TV show or licensing the cartoon or the Web site or whatever—to the creative part, which is the part I know. I don't try to program the Web or to be a director or editor or sound guy on the show.

L2L: Information overload and competing priorities are huge frustrations for managers. You get hundreds of e-mail messages a day, and you have to meet daily deadlines. How do you manage your time and your creative process?

SA: I tend to be really good at time management. This is also the business part, the hard wiring of the brain. It turns out that when you get massive amounts of e-mail it all falls into about 20 different types of comments, and the speed at which you can read them is phenomenal. Also, I've got software that searches for keywords so it picks out messages I know I have to deal with at a higher level of priority.

Let me give you a few other tips. I don't answer the phone before 10 A.M. And I do most of my creative work from about 7 to 10. That's the great thing about working at home: no one can drop in to my cubicle. If I don't answer my phone, I am unreachable. I had a pager for a while—got rid of it. And when you have control over your own schedule, you can do busywork types of things when your mind can only do those things and do creative things when you're at your peak. I just don't ever mix those.

L2L: Do you have heroes, people you admire or look to for inspiration?

SA: Yes. Lately I've been reading about great geniuses through time, like Isaac Newton and Richard Feynman. I also like Bill Gates. Maybe the fact that he's so demonized appeals to me on some level. But the thing I can't escape—this is the economist part of my hardwiring—is to compare Bill Gates to Mother Teresa. Now, on the surface, it's hahahahaha—he's evil, she's good. End of story. Mother Teresa worked her whole life with lepers, and she left a great legacy. Bill Gates wrote one check for $100 million to give vaccinations to children. He helped a thousand times more people than Mother Teresa, and he did it in the time it took to write a check.

You can argue about specific tactics or things that Microsoft has done or not done. But for the most part, Gates has really big goals and he works on them very diligently and—this is the interesting part—he works on them like a scientist. He doesn't work on them like a Mother Teresa. He's not the marketing guy, he's the problem solver, he's the game winner. If his wealth doubles every 10 years, he could become the first trillionaire! And he says he wants to give it away. Let's say he does, and he does it the same way he gave away the first little bit: he picked something the government just wasn't going to do. It had immediate, amazing lifesaving impact. Did 10 million people live because he wrote that check? Possibly. So he is picking out those places where only he can make a difference and have long-term benefits and is not just washing the feet of a leper. That's a holy thing to do, but when you're done, all you have is a leper with clean feet. I know it's a totally unpopular point of view, but you can't escape the math of it.

L2L: You're not far from the point in your career where a lot of successful entrepreneurs start thinking about their legacy—what they want to do for others. Do you have any such plans?

SA: I do, yes. I just created a company that makes a nutritious food item called the "Dilberito." It's a microwavable burrito with 100 percent of your 23 daily vitamin and mineral needs.

On the surface, this doesn't sound like a big deal. But the biggest cause of illness and death in the United States is poor diet. That means the single biggest opportunity to improve health is by improving diet. I assumed, as most people do, that if you eat "right" you get most of what your body needs. But check the nutrition labels on your food. You could eat a wheelbarrow full of food before you got your vitamin and mineral requirements.

I'd call what I'm doing enlightened capitalism. I'm investing in a nutrition product—as opposed to making a new kind of hubcap—because improved nutrition will make life on earth better. I chose capitalism as my engine because it's self-sustaining and relatively efficient. And it's something I'm good at. My economics training doesn't allow me to make the clean distinctions between charity and capitalism that most people do. In any case, I plan to rid myself of whatever wealth I've created before I die, so in my case the only differences between capitalism and philanthropy are timing and effectiveness.

L2L: Scott, we started by talking about gurus, so let's finish with this. Some people view you as a kind of spokesman for our times. What do you make of the impact that your work has had on others?

SA: I've never been comfortable with the "spokesman" label. I think *Dilbert*'s impact has less to do with what it says than what it hears. I sense a collective relief from *Dilbert* readers that their unspoken frustrations have been heard. Sometimes people just need to know someone is listening.

Scott Adams is the creator of *Dilbert*, which appears in 1,900 newspapers around the world, and author of four best-selling books, including *The Dilbert Principle*, which has sold 1.5 million copies since 1996. His publications, prime-time TV show, Web site, and 700 licensed products have made Adams the head of a virtual company with an estimated $200 million in annual revenues.

5

Economically Correct Leadership

James O'Toole, Bruce Pasternack, and Jeffrey W. Bennett

A global study reveals the inefficiency of systems with overly central leadership. The amount of information is limited, and the risk of error is high. Overcontrol saps initiative and fosters bureaucratic behavior, whereas shared responsibility generates diverse input, cooperation, and entrepreneurial behavior. The authors offer a model of leadership based on decentralization of decision making, allocation of resources based on economically correct market mechanisms, minimizing organizational activities, entrepreneurial incentives and accountability, and unambiguous values. This model frees leaders to communicate the visions, values, missions, and strategies of their organizations; to develop others' competence and reward performance; and to create and maintain systems in which others can work effectively.

In September 2000, United Nations Secretary General Kofi Annan addressed the General Assembly at the end of the Millennium Summit of world leaders. He concluded that if only

Editor's note: There is risk in any high-performance organization. Enron now provides different illustrations from those employed in the article, written in 2000.

one thing had been learned in the 20th century, it is that "centrally planned systems don't work." As recently as a decade ago, such an assertion would have been cause for U.N. delegates to walk out of the assembly hall in mass protest—and not just the Communist Bloc delegates but representatives of many Third World countries as well.

But now the world clearly has changed: Even the ambassadors of Russia and China were unfazed by Annan's conclusion. Many seemed to be nodding (or perhaps nodding off) at the recitation of what, in a remarkably short time, has morphed into a self-evident truth: *The collective intelligence of the market is greater than the directive smarts of one individual (or cadre of commissars).* And that truth doesn't apply just to economics. While some in Beijing (and in Singapore) remain unconvinced, most of the world also has bought the notion that political decisions in which citizens participate are better than fiats of dictators.

In an ongoing study of the leadership practices of corporate members of the World Economic Forum (known for their annual gathering in Davos, Switzerland), we are documenting the beginnings of a similar sea change in the way business organizations think about their structure and governance. Using in-depth interviews and a survey of over 6,000 executives and managers in Asia, Europe, and North America, Booz-Allen & Hamilton is creating a global database of effective (and ineffective) leadership practices. While we have seen cases in which an all-powerful business leader has compelled an organization to achieve a focused end (such as American Airlines' Robert Crandall, an acknowledged master of change by command), we also have found that such leadership is unstable in the long run.

The Old Way of Leadership

Solo corporate leadership has become inefficient and ineffective for much the same reasons that Kremlin dictators ultimately destroyed the system they attempted to control. In businesses with overly centralized leadership, the risk of serious error is extremely high. No one, no matter how gifted, can be right all the time, and no one has all the information required to make every important decision, particularly in large organizations. When one or a handful of people are making all the calls, over time resources become misallocated, opportunities missed, and innovation stifled. Over-control saps initiative and fosters routinized, bureaucratic behavior. Organizations dependent on a single individual—even a brilliant individual—are at risk when that individual leaves, retires, or dies. Harold Geneen could single-handedly run ITT, but after him that conglomerate crumbled like the Warsaw Pact after the demise of the Soviet dictatorship.

That said, we cannot deny the success of the charismatic leadership of Larry Ellison at Oracle, Sandy Weill at CitiGroup, Scott McNealy at Sun Microsystems, and, in particular, that of McNealy's mentor, Jack Welch at General Electric. There is good reason why these powerful individuals are cited in the business press as examples of the standard, one-man model of corporate leadership: the companies they run have impressive financial records. Ellison has demonstrated, while centralizing decision-making authority for development, marketing, and pricing, that he could turn Oracle into the world's leading producer of databases and Internet-based software. Weill has shown that he can produce extremely fast growth through an acquisition strategy that he himself leads and executes. At Sun the CEO is so powerful that, in the public eye, the company is Scott

McNealy. And starting in the 1980s the all-powerful Welch became the iconic corporate leadership figure of the age when he single-handedly forced G.E.'s managers to undergo a revolution in corporate practices—at a time when they were content to bask in their manifest success.

The New Shape of Leadership

Given the performance of such storied individuals, it is no wonder that leadership in this country is still represented in the business press in the guise of personalities.

Yet, below and beyond this personification of leadership lies a pattern of emerging behavior. At General Electric, in fact, Jack Welch worked overtime to build leadership bench strength throughout his organization—seeking, as he prepared to retire, to institutionalize leadership in the company's structure and systems. Even in Asia, where corporate power often is centralized in the hands of an owner and founder, we see a countertrend in which large, publicly traded companies in Korea, India, and Japan now seek to make leadership institutional—as opposed to individual—by cascading power down the organizational hierarchy. Since the death of Akio Morita, Sony has moved to a more decentralized leadership model, and as the legendary CEO of Fuji-Xerox, Yotaro Kobayashi, prepared to retire, he worked to make that company far less dependent on any individual in the future.

Lost in the hype surrounding the high-profile, do-it-all-themselves leaders of the e-biz and high-tech industries is the fact that some of the most impressive corporate performances are being turned in by three companies that were traditionally in decidedly unglamorous industries: Corning, Continental Airlines, and Enron. Significantly, many key leadership tasks in those companies are institutionalized in organizational systems, practices, and cultures. Leadership in these firms is not a solo act, an aria sung by a prima donna CEO; instead, it is a shared responsibility, a chorus of diverse and complementary voices. Without a single, charismatic (or commanding) leader goading them on, individuals down the line act more like owners and entrepreneurs than like hired hands. To an unusual degree, these companies are chock-full o' leaders—men and women who take responsibility for financial performance and managing risk, people at all levels who take initiative to solve problems and even to start new businesses.

A Rational Market Model

Significantly, the emerging model of leadership is in keeping with principles of accepted economic theory. For example, economists put their trust in markets rather than structures because people are rational (and organizations only rarely so). While the details of their business models vary, these three companies adhere to a few organizational basics that true capitalists celebrate in principle but often ignore in their own companies.

• *Decentralization*. Because "Better information leads to better decisions," decision making is delegated to the lowest appropriate level (where the best information resides), unless there is a compelling reason for making it elsewhere.

• *Market mechanisms*. "The market is the most efficient process for allocating resources." Thus central planning staffs and powerful budget offices are shunned in favor of market-style processes that allow scarce resources to flow to individuals or departments based on an assessment of risk and reward (for example, to a division that is willing to bid most for a day of salesforce time).

• *Minimalism.* The corporation engages only in those activities that cannot be bought more cheaply from others in the market, and those few things that require scale or technical expertise.

• *Ownership.* Since "entrepreneurial behavior is desirable," the rule is to fix accountability wherever possible by making people at all levels feel the consequences of their own decisions. Need it be said that "people respond to incentives"?

• *Rule of law.* As newly democratic Russia is discovering, capitalist nations need the rule of law for markets to operate effectively. Ditto companies. Hence, to make it simpler for people to manage in complex organizations, leaders need to establish a few unambiguous values that everyone understands—and that leaders themselves uphold without exception.

Exercising Restraint

Why, when we move from society to individual enterprises, are these principles so often honored in the breach? The reason is simple: the leader's ego gets in the way. Since nearly all CEOs like to think of themselves as the sort of all-knowing, tough, and take-charge leader who gets profiled on the cover of *Forbes*, they are tempted to centralize authority, to make all important capital allocation decisions themselves (Larry Ellison is said to review all decisions involving sums above $50,000) and, in general, to structure their organizations as if there was need for only one entrepreneur.

Yet our research shows that companies whose operations are predicated on market principles require complementary, decentralized leadership behavior to be fully effective—particularly in the long term. For example, such successful CEOs as Enron's Kenneth Lay, Continental's Gordon Bethune, and Corning's Roger Ackerman resist the ego-satisfying (and media-approved) urge to lead by push—particularly when times are rough and the faint-hearted call for "a strong hand at the helm." They understand that reverting to a Stalinist model of leadership would only destroy their own credibility—and their organizations' overall capacity to be self-governing and self-renewing. Instead, they use the pull of incentives linked to purpose. They maintain the discipline to trust in people and markets. They understand that people—and markets—can be cultivated but not controlled.

The difficulty of exercising leadership restraint is acknowledged by economist Oliver Williamson, who compares it to Odysseus' having to "lash himself to the mast" to avoid being seduced by the song of the Sirens. Presumably, modern organizational Sirens sing an irresistible refrain that goes something like, "*You* must manage everything. *You* must control everything. . . ."

Disciplined adherence to the economic model focuses the executives' attention on the true requirements of effective leadership and away from managerial tasks that should, in any event, be delegated. Leaders like Lay, Bethune, and Ackerman practice executive restraint—they have a bias against intervention, particularly in tactical decisions. They create conditions that are predictable—as opposed to arbitrary—and they build trust in the process. But that doesn't mean they create static systems—or that they themselves are uninvolved. When the inevitable exceptions to their few organizing principles force them to make a decision, they decide clearly and promptly—but in a way that sets clear precedent for the future, instead of creating the need to decide again tomorrow. For example, a few years back car maker Renault experienced a bad case of that common bureaucratic conflict known as siloing or stovepiping, in which manufacturing, sales, and marketing failed to engage in necessary cross-functional co-operation. Carlos Ghosn, then COO, stepped in and changed the structure, measurement, and reward systems, creating cross-functional, self-managing teams, each fully responsible for all decisions relating to a particular piece of a car: power train, interior, body, and so forth. Moreover, when such leaders are successful they find they need to make fewer and fewer decisions themselves because they will have spent as much as a third of their time developing other leaders who, in turn, make more (and better) decisions. "Economically correct" leaders also encourage conflict resolution at lower levels—instead of tolerating the inefficient habit of kicking all problems upstairs.

Spending Time Wisely

What do they do with the rest of their time? The most effective leaders we have studied spend over half of their time communicating the visions, strategies, values, and missions of their organizations, and rewarding managers down the line for translating those generalities into the specific behavior required to realize overall objectives. They spend time selecting and developing a leadership team. Finally, they create and maintain systems in which others can do their work effectively. Since markets are all about rationality, these technical and organizational systems must be transparent and provide the information, resources, and authority so that followers can get their work done without interference.

Here are some examples of what economically correct leadership means in practice: In the mid-1990s, Roger Ackerman began a change process that has led to the total revamping of

Corning's core technologies. He asked 300 employees from all levels to identify opportunities for process and product improvements and to initiate activities based on their own ideas. The actual work of change was done by those same people, organized in teams that they led themselves. Top management limited its role to setting stretch goals, holding the teams accountable, and communicating the purpose of the change effort. Another example of dispersed leadership: a $3 billion acquisition recently was executed by a third-echelon Corning manager.

When Gordon Bethune took over at Continental in 1994, the company had recently been in Chapter 11 bankruptcy and was ranked last in its industry on every measure that mattered. To turn the company around, Bethune chose the radical strategy of meeting customer needs. To get Continental's planes to arrive on time, Bethune offered all employees a bonus check of $65 each month the company ranked among the nation's top five airlines in on-time performance. Bethune set the goal, but he left it up to the employees to creatively come up with ways to achieve it. At the end of the first month, the company had moved from tenth to seventh place on the government's on-time rankings. The next month they hit fourth place (and got their first bonus checks, cut with the words "Thank you for helping us to be on time" printed on the bottom.) The following month, they hit first place—and have stayed there rather consistently. What did Bethune do as an economically correct leader? He says, "The challenge is to keep people focused." And linking customer needs to the self-interest of employees is the best way to keep people focused on their real job.

In the 1980s, Enron was a slow-growing Texas-based gas pipeline company. Today it is a global world-beater engaged in such fast-growth industries as power marketing and bandwidth trading. The change came about as the result of CEO Lay's decision to create an environment in which bright young MBAs with entrepreneurial instincts would have "the resources to succeed and freedom to fail without penalty." Over the years, Enron has recruited nearly a thousand new leaders to create and run their own businesses—and to have a healthy financial stake in their success. To cope with constant change, people are free to move around in the company as new growth areas emerge or once-promising areas dry up. To make this work, Lay has implemented a system in which employees who change jobs don't have their salaries lowered—even if they move into a lower-level job than the one they held previously. Because even titles are portable, executive VPs in slow-growing businesses are willing to take second-tier technical jobs in areas where they can make a greater contribution to the corporation. And what does Lay do? He creates the environment in which the entrepreneurial efforts of thousands of employees can make him a successful leader and Enron's shareholders wealthy.

Making Strategy Effective

Paradoxically, what seems natural in theory requires counterintuitive behavior on the part of many practitioners. For example, our research shows that the performance of few companies meets the aspirations of their leaders (and none fulfills its true potential). When leaders are asked why, they typically explain this gulf between performance and expectations as a shortcoming of vision or strategy—or lay it at the feet of people down the line whose behavior or skill is inconsistent with policies proclaimed on high.

While a sound strategy is necessary for superior performance, most strategies can be quickly copied (and many are little more than statements of aspiration that offer little real direction to employees). The gap between performance and aspiration is usually caused by the way an organization shapes the decisions of individual managers and employees. Organizational performance is the collective result of all the effort and activity that goes on inside a firm, and that behavior is determined by the operating environment—that is, the system in which people work.

Most leaders acknowledge the importance of such organizational systems as

- Goal setting
- Performance appraisal
- Recruiting
- Knowledge transfer
- Capital allocations
- Communications

Yet surprisingly few leaders know the degree to which such systems lead to alignment between strategy and behavior. And even fewer understand the ways in which such systems work to encourage (or impede) innovation and initiative—that is, the organizational adaptability needed to cope with an ever-changing environment. Indeed, the sources of organizational misalignment and maladaptation are so numerous, diverse, complex, and cross-cutting that they are hard to identify and thus are seldom the focus of concerted leadership actions.

We have learned that it is exactly such organizational systems that drive performance—and it is such systems that leaders like Lay, Ackerman, and Bethune spend almost all their time creating and maintaining. In our World Economic Forum research we applied a standardized survey that helps leaders to assess which systems in their organizations are most effective at driving performance, and to assess the effectiveness of those systems relative to those in other companies. The survey instrument asks respondents at all hierarchical levels to score their organization on 65 measures of behavior. Instead of measuring attitudes, the instrument asks respondents to use its seven-point scale to score the degree to which leaders do specific things (for example, "hold people accountable for their performance"). By using this diagnostic method, leaders pinpoint the systemic sources of alignment and adaptability in their organizations and, in the manner of CEOs Lay, Ackerman, and Bethune, then build agendas that focus their leadership actions on those few things that really influence performance.

As it turns out, all complex organizations contain built-in conflicts and disincentives that cause people to behave in ways that are inconsistent with overall strategy and goals. These relatively low-level points of conflict (for example, when business units are asked to cooperate on one hand but are rewarded for maximizing their own profits on the other) are not apparent to top-level leaders but, when added up, significantly affect corporate performance. Thus the most effective point of leadership leverage is to identify and unblock impediments to group performance. Surveys, focus groups, and other tools can identify such counterproductive decision points. Then a detailed analysis of the incentives that influence the managers making these decisions often reveals the sources of misdirection. Armed with that knowledge, new and more rational rules governing who makes what decisions can be created to better align behavior throughout the organization with the leader's overall strategy.

In sum, effective leadership is not about charisma or the exercise of power; instead, it entails the creation of information and incentive systems that allow others to make decisions that, cumulatively, advance organization objectives. The role of leaders in an economically correct enterprise is less about "showing the way" to sheeplike followers, and more about providing the context in which capable individuals can find their own best paths to meeting overall goals. Senior leaders thus create the environment that motivates good decision making: they recruit competent people, develop them, give them appropriate tools, authority, and resources, hold them accountable, and reward their "right" behavior. They focus on organizational results rather than on personal position. It is the lasting power of those results, not the imputed power of the individual, that defines real leadership.

James O'Toole is research professor at the University of Southern California's Center for Effective Organizations and chair of Booz-Allen & Hamilton's Board of Academic Advisors. He has published 13 books and more than 70 articles focusing on political philosophy, planning, corporate culture and leadership. His most recent book is *Leadership A to Z*.

Bruce Pasternack is senior vice president of Booz-Allen & Hamilton and managing partner of its San Francisco office. He leads the firm's Organization and Strategic Leadership practice and serves on the Advisory Council of Stanford University's Graduate School of Business. He is coauthor of *The Centerless Corporation*.

Jeffrey W. Bennett is vice president of the Consumer and Health Group of Booz-Allen & Hamilton, based in Cleveland. His recent work focused on strategy and organization, primarily in the consumer packaged goods and consumer durables industries.

The authors acknowledge the contributions to this piece made by their Booz-Allen & Hamilton colleagues Karen Van Nuys, Tom Persteiner, Steve Hedlund, and Tom Williams.

6

Laws of the Jungle and the New Laws of Business

Richard Tanner Pascale

Like organisms, organizations must avoid equilibrium, which makes them less responsive to external change and threat. Because homogeneous organisms (and organizations) are more vulnerable, they must cultivate diversity. They must move toward the edge of chaos, experiment, and self-organize to take advantage of opportunities. The three phases of change are (1) experimentation and disorder, (2) doing away with established practices and people, and (3) articulating a vision of the future that leads to a new state or condition. In this process, it is important not to dictate behavior, which can cause resistance, but to design so that things flow in the intended direction.

Two imperatives govern survival in many industries today. The first requires agility in the face of high levels of strategic ambiguity. The second is a shift in culture and capability from slow, deliberate organizations to forms that behave like living

Adapted from *Surfing the Edge of Chaos*. Reprinted with permission of Crown Business.

organisms, fostering entrepreneurial initiatives, consolidating learning, and moving rapidly to exploit winning positions in the marketplace.

One of the best places to learn how to meet these challenges is by looking at life itself. Over many millions of years, nature has devised strategies for coping with prolonged periods of gradual change and occasional cataclysms in which only the most agile survive. This latter condition, in particular, teaches us much about how species deal with turmoil. Four principles, running counter to many current and conventional management beliefs, stand out as the primary lessons from life.

1. Equilibrium is a precursor to death. When a living system is in a state of equilibrium, it is less responsive to changes occurring around it. This places it at maximum risk.

2. In the face of threat, or when galvanized by a compelling opportunity, living things move toward the edge of chaos. This condition evokes higher levels of mutation and experimentation, making fresh new solutions more likely.

3. Once this excitation takes place, the components of living systems self-organize, and new forms and repertoires emerge from the turmoil. This property of life is called "self-organization and emergence."

4. Living systems cannot be directed along a linear path. Unforeseen consequences are inevitable. The challenge is to learn how to disturb them toward the desired outcome and then course-correct as the outcome unfolds.

Properly employed, these four principles allow enterprises to thrive and revitalize themselves. In contrast, the more familiar machine-age principles, while enduring, often prompt the stagnation and decline of traditional enterprises that face discontinuous change. The choice is that simple and that stark.

The assertion *equilibrium is death* derives from an obscure but important law of cybernetics, the Law of Requisite Variety, which states that the survival of any organism depends on its capacity to *cultivate* (not just tolerate) variety in its internal structure. Failure to do so leads to inability to cope successfully with variety when it is introduced from outside. For example, fish in a bowl can swim, breed, obtain food with minimal effort, safe from predators. But, as aquarium owners know, such fish are excruciatingly sensitive to the slightest perturbations. Fish in the sea have to work much harder to sustain themselves and evade many threats. But because they cope with more variation, they are more robust when faced with change.

The lessons of Requisite Variety make us uneasy. Equilibrium is associated with balance—a good thing, surely. Disequilibrium is balance gone haywire. But consider the industrial landscape in this context. For a greater part of the last century, dazzling new technologies (electronics, engineered materials, computers and bioengineering) opened vast frontiers of commerce in which traditional management models flourished. Add to that 55 years without destructive global conflict. One result was the emergence of industrial economies with vast wealth, spending power, and consumer appetites. A good part of the 20th century, excluding the Great Depression and the war years, may be regarded as an era of low-hanging fruit. Outdated approaches to management haven't changed because they didn't have to. True to Woody Allen's quip that 80 percent of success is just showing up, lumbering corporations thrived because they showed up; their lack of agility was not a significant drawback given their advantages of scale and the cornucopia of economic opportunity they had to feast upon.

Then some unlikely start-ups, borne on the wings of new business models, proceeded to spoil the party. The newcomers—companies like Enron, Amazon.com, Southwest Airlines, Qwest, Home Depot, and Nokia—ran rings around traditional companies mired in comfortable equilibrium.

A qualification is warranted here. The extent to which balance or equilibrium is a precursor of disaster must be assessed in the context of scale and time. At small scales and in short time frames, equilibrium can be desirable. But over long intervals and on very large scales, it becomes hazardous. Why? Because the environment in which an organism (or organization) lives is always changing. At times, it is turbulent. Prolonged equilibrium dulls an organism's senses and saps its ability to arouse itself appropriately in the face of danger.

So why don't all living systems spiral into the thrall of equilibrium and die? Because two countervailing forces are at work. One is the *threat of death* (through the eternal Darwinian struggle for survival); the other is the *promise of sex* (that is, recombinations that introduce genetic diversity).

One of Darwin's most important contributions was his observation that species (by which we mean all members of a living system) do not evolve of their own accord. Rather, they change because of the forces, indeed threats, imposed on them from the environment. Life scientists call these "selection pressures." Selection pressures intensify during periods of radical upheaval. Most species, when challenged to adapt too far from their origins, are unable to do so and disappear. But nature is a fertile and indifferent mother, more dedicated to proliferating life in general than to the perpetuation of any particular species. From the vantage point of the larger system, selection pressures constantly enforce an ecological upgrade. The mutations that survive fit better in the new environment.

Reflecting on the competitive corporate landscape of the past decade or two, we can readily identify with Darwin's insights. New rivals are constantly converging on the same market opportunity and clamber relentlessly over one another toward a better position in the economic food chain. Whole sectors decline or disappear entirely. Office-supply stores are swept away by Staples, and the largest and best-established bookseller, Barnes & Noble, is badly shaken by Amazon.com. The examples speak to the ubiquity of selection pressures as they play out on the corporate landscape. There are no safe havens. From cell phones to cotton seeds, soap to software, it is a Darwinian jungle out there, and it isn't getting easier.

Sex is nature's second defense against stagnation. Organisms become more vulnerable as they become more homogeneous. To thwart homogeneity, nature relies on the rich structural recombinations triggered by sexual reproduction. Sex is decisively superior to evolution's other major alternative for species replication: fission.

Sexual reproduction maximizes diversity. Chromosome combinations are randomly matched in variant pairings, generating permutations and variety in offspring. Harmful diseases and parasites find it harder to breach the diverse defenses of a population generated by sexual reproduction. Microbes equipped to pick the locks of one generation of a particular species discover that the cellular tumblers have been changed in the next. When the bubonic plague swept through Europe in the 14th century, it killed 30 percent of the population. Subsequent waves of the deadly contagion claimed only a fraction of that number. Antibodies passed on to most of the progeny of the first wave's survivors made subsequent generations less susceptible when the bacteria returned for an encore.

Exchanges of DNA within social systems are unfortunately not nearly as reliable as those driven by the mechanics of reproductive biology. True, organizations can hire from outside, bring senior officers into frequent contact with iconoclasts from the ranks, or require engineers and designers to meet with disgruntled customers and listen to them. But the enemy of these mechanisms for exchanging metaphoric DNA is, of course, the existing social order. Like the body's immune defense system, the social order identifies foreign influences and seeks to neutralize them.

Xerox PARC (Palo Alto Research Center) is a case in point. The Xerox R&D lab invented ALTO (which many regard as the first personal computer), the first commercial mouse, Ethernet (predecessor of the Internet), many of the basic protocols of the Internet, client-server architecture, laser printing, and flat-panel displays, to name a few of its numerous contributions. Yet because the mainstream organization could not rouse itself from the deadening equilibrium of the copier business, it did not recognize nor incorporate the new DNA in its midst. Result: Xerox remained in the backwater of the major wealth-creating opportunities of the past 30 years. This legacy will surely warrant its place in the corporate hall of shame.

Equilibrium enforcers—persistent social norms, corporate values, and orthodox beliefs about the business—often nullify the sought-after advantages of diversity. An executive team may recruit an outsider to gain diversity, then regress into behavior that nullifies the advantage by listening stereotypically. ("There goes the techie again!" "Ah—the feminist point of view.") The new token "genetic material" often finds itself frozen out of important informal discussions in which the real business gets done. Of course, humans have an important advantage. As self-knowing and intelligent entities, companies, at least in theory, are capable of recognizing danger (or opportunity) in advance and mobilizing to take appropriate action. They can wield the power of intention. To a greater extent than other species, humans and their constructs can lift themselves by their anticipatory bootstraps.

Nature is at its innovative best near the edge of chaos. The edge of chaos is a condition, not a location. It is a permeable, intermediate state through which order and disorder flow, not a finite line of demarcation. Moving to the edge of chaos creates upheaval but not dissolution. That's why the *edge* of chaos is so important. The edge is not the abyss. It's the sweet spot for productive change.

Innovations rarely emerge from systems high in order and stability. Systems in equilibrium lose diversity and give rise to the sorts of problems one encounters in incestuous communities and centrally planned economies. On the other hand, completely chaotic systems—riots, the stock market crash of 1929, or the Chinese Cultural Revolution of 1965–1976—are too hot to handle. Developments must wait until things settle down a bit.

When a complex adaptive system is moved toward the edge of chaos—when hurricanes and typhoons roil the deep seas, or fires rage through forests or prairies—the potential for generativity is maximized. Hurricanes recharge the oceans with oxygen and nutrients, and replenish carbon dioxide in the atmosphere. Fires cleanse a forest and make room for new life. In fact, fires have been found to be absolutely essential to the regeneration of the tall grass prairies of the Great Plains. The biodiversity inherent in prairies is stifled when fires are suppressed.

Andy Grove, former chairman of Intel, had a long-standing appreciation of the realm near chaos. He embraced it as part of his executive toolkit. His skills at the edge were honed by incidents in Intel's history: the forced march from semiconductors into memory chips as Intel shifted from a me-too clone of Texas Instruments and Fairchild to define a distinct competitive advantage; the retreat from chips to microprocessors (when Asian price reductions and Japanese quality destroyed Intel's market niche); and, more recently, the branding of the Pentium chip, which alienated Intel's largest customers (the PC manufacturers) by establishing a retail franchise with end users.

Microprocessors, the mother lode of information technology, are not only the expensive brains of personal computers and workstations, they are becoming increasingly important to intelligent automotive controls, cell phones, and consumer electronics of all kinds. The wealth-creating potential of microprocessors has been a magnet to Intel's competitors. Each new Intel offering sparks an arms race with clone suppliers seeking to introduce a cheaper alternative. Instead of three-year life cycles (from premium to commodity pricing), prices have been collapsing in 12 to 18 months. Grove's prescription was to move the organization quickly from denial to acceptance of the change. Grove states:

"First, you must experiment and let chaos reign. That's important because you're not likely to successfully stumble on the answer at the first sign of trouble. Rather, you have to let the business units struggle and watch the dissonance grow in the company. As this unfolds, you enter the second phase of change, which I describe as the Valley of Death. Doing away with established practice and established people—tearing apart before you can put together something new—is not fun. Talking prematurely about changes that disrupt people's lives and are not truly believed can undermine efforts before you really know what you're doing. But once they are in place, it is essential for leadership to speak clearly about what the changes mean and what the organization is going to do. At this point, you are at the other side of the Valley of Death and you can describe the future that lies ahead."

Over recent years, top executives at Monsanto, Shell, and the U.S. Army who sought to use the edge of chaos to spur innovation and learning have drawn considerable media attention. Monsanto and Shell intentionally overloaded the system with initiatives that cut across geographies and hierarchical levels, culminating with highly visible, real-time business reviews that put both the senior executive team and the lower-level professionals presenting their ideas on the line. For insiders, this all felt very much like the edge of chaos. The U.S. Army takes entire battalions, 3,000 soldiers from generals through privates, and subjects them to two weeks of combat against a superior "enemy." Every maneuver is monitored by video, audio, and laser tracking devices. Twenty-hour working days, extreme conditions in the Mojave Desert, and disciplined After Action Reviews (armed with hard data on what actually happened) offer no place to hide. All this is orchestrated to push the units to the edge of chaos, leading to deep learning and desired levels of tactical improvisation.

But why *the edge*, many ask. Wouldn't it suffice to disturb equilibrium but give the edge of chaos a wide berth? Edges are important to life; in fact, people are drawn to them. When you are in the middle of things it is much harder to get your bearings, let alone experience the adrenaline rush of "pushing the envelope."

The visual cortex of the brain directs your eyes to look for edges, helping you distinguish figure from background and consequently to get your bearings. Living systems generally push up against the edge as a way of determining how much turbulence is enough. The yellow light of a traffic signal triggers motorists' response. They either apply the brakes or accelerate through the intersection. The yellow light is analogous to the edge. It stimulates heightened awareness and generates a burst of adrenaline and mental activity. Drivers strive to avoid ending up in cross traffic in the intersection—analogous to outright chaos.

Consider how most of us cope with deadlines. When deadlines are far in the future, we experience no urgency and may even feel complacent. And if the deadline is imminent and we know we cannot meet it, we experience unproductive stress and mental gridlock. Too much stress causes us to oversimplify, to jump to conclusions, become paralyzed, or default to old habits and prior success routines. We learn from experience how to make constructive use of an upcoming time limit; we know that an unmet deadline will evoke an optimal level of adrenaline, tension, and creativity. Many people experience their most productive moments near this temporal edge of chaos.

The trick, of course, is to navigate close to the edge of chaos without falling into it. There are three essential navigation devices:

1. *Attractors*, analogous to a compass, orient a living system in one direction and provide the impetus to migrate out of the comfort zone. Robert Shapiro, CEO of Monsanto, demonstrated the practical application of attractors by generating a compelling aspiration within the ranks to become the world's leading life sciences company. The attractor was strong enough to mobilize

the company to leave behind its safe legacy as an established manufacturer of bulk chemicals.

2. *Amplifying and damping feedback* serve like the throttle and brake of a propulsion system. They cause a process to accelerate or to slow down. John Browne, chairman and formerly managing director of British Petroleum's Oil Exploration (BPX) unit, made excellent use of amplification devices to push that system out of equilibrium and toward the edge of chaos. He used damping controls to prevent BPX from spiraling into confusion and nonperformance.

3. *Fitness landscape* is a term used by ecologists and other life scientists to map the relative competitive advantage of species. Such landscapes provide a useful device for visualizing today's competition—certainly superior to the traditional two-dimensional Strengths Weaknesses Opportunities Threats analysis one encounters in conventional strategic assessments. Monsanto exemplifies how an organization can move over its fitness landscape, modifying the topography as it goes. Monsanto succeeded in climbing one fitness peak to become the leading life sciences company. But almost immediately the landscape changed. In the face of European outcry over bioengineered foods, Monsanto was caught flat-footed. Its very success had placed it in the crosshairs of activists seeking a "public enemy."

On fitness landscapes, higher degrees of fitness are depicted by linear height on the landscape. Loss of fitness is visualized as going downhill in this three-dimensional territory. Thus, when a threatened species, such as the North American coyote, is driven from its traditional habitat by human extermination programs, it descends the fitness landscape toward the edge of chaos. It must learn to cope with different terrain, climate, and rivals, and to find new sources of food. Coyotes have become urbanized in many sections of the country. Once established in a new territory, a coyote begins to master its new environment. This adaptation may, in fact, lead to overall prospects for survival that are better than those in the original habitat. In this context, the coyote's fitness has increased. It has carved out a niche on a superior fitness peak in the foothills above Malibu and Beverly Hills.

Biologists describe a species' or population's struggle to secure a niche as a long climb uphill, where "uphill" means better adaptation. When a species reaches a subsidiary peak (called a *local optimum*) on the fitness landscape, it may choose to remain there. Biologists call this perch on the fitness landscape a basin of attraction—a rest stop during the eternal competitive journey in which equilibrium is only temporarily restored.

Species become stranded on intermediate peaks or basins of attraction. Because there are no suspension bridges to get to the higher peaks on the horizon, the organism must "go down to go up." (This image is useful because most organisms don't do this voluntarily.) To do so, there must be sufficient internal unrest and instability; otherwise, an organism would not opt to leave its intermediate peak and suffer the indignities of the valley: low margins, undifferentiated products, customer defections, loss of competitive advantage—on the gamble of reaching a higher perch on the fitness landscape. And the apparent desirability of climbing a new peak can change radically if the environment changes. Traditional retailers such as Barnes & Noble sit on a "local peak" of the bookselling landscape and set their sights on what appears to be the more desirable peak of e-commerce in this example, the peak occupied by Amazon.com. Barnes & Noble plots a course to get to that peak. Along the way, e-commerce attracts an enormous amount of media attention and wanna-be contenders. The excitement solidifies Amazon.com as the business platform of the future, a label that publicly increases the value of its franchise. And Barnes & Noble, as it strives to build an e-commerce channel of its own, is still rooted in its lower peak because of its embedded base as a traditional bookseller. Amazon.com's peak seems to grow higher, until, perhaps, the hype about e-commerce begins to slacken. Investor interest diminishes, stock prices fall, and e-retailers like Amazon.com (which have yet to show a profit) face a day of reckoning. Retrenchment takes place as they endeavor to do so. For Barnes & Noble, still at midcourse in the journey, the new peak loses altitude and becomes less desirable.

No illustration of how the business landscape can change is more compelling than Monsanto's. The initial success with genetically improved crops (and the speed at which these innovations were adopted in the United States) catapulted the enterprise to a new peak—and inadvertently put it into the epicenter of a public relations nightmare. Monsanto was the darling of Wall Street one day, the instigator of "Frankenstein Foods" the next. How this turnaround emerged is illustrative of the cascades and avalanches that can occur in living systems.

The third principle of nature, *self-organization and emergence*, captures two sides of the same coin of life. *Self-organization* is the tendency of certain (but not all) systems operating far from equilibrium to shift to a new state when their constituent elements generate unlikely combinations. When systems become sufficiently populated and properly interconnected, the interactions assemble themselves into a new order: proteins into cells, cells into organs, organs into organisms, organisms into societies. Simple parts networked together can undergo a metamorphosis. A single ant can't drive off a bee. A single brain cell is useless—but a few tens of millions of them can perform miracles. *Emergence* is the outcome of all this: a new state or condition. A colony of fire ants has emergent capabilities and constitutes an organism weighing 20 kilograms, with 20 million mouths and stings. A jazz ensemble creates an emergent sound that no one could imagine from listening to the individual instruments. Two hundred years ago, Adam Smith was on the scent of these insights. As one of the pioneers of the new discipline of economics, he called our attention to the "invisible hand" and its aggregate effects as a mercantile force. But Smith recognized that individual choice did not explain everything since individuals, as members of communities, generate fiduciary relationships and dependencies. All this, he noted, sums to a more complex *emergent* phenomenon: an economy.

The principle of self-organization and emergence resonates with a new consensus that is forming within the ranks of management: companies with talent and the instincts to mobilize distributed intelligence, innovate, and collaborate can commercialize ideas and seize the high ground before slower rivals even spot the new hill. By inspiring frontline personnel to improvise as quasi-independent agents and generate customer solutions without stultifying central controls, small breakthroughs can swell into formidable business enterprises and social movements.

A great way to grasp the power of this principle is to witness the effects of its absence. On January 2–3, 1999, a blizzard closed Detroit Airport, canceling many outbound flights. Snowplows kept runways open and a good number of inbound planes were able to land. Most carriers—United, TWA, and American—managed to bring their planes to the gates and offload passengers with modest delays. But that is not what happened with Northwest Airlines.

In perhaps one of the greatest public relations debacles in airline history, Northwest's overwhelmed ground staff seemed paralyzed in a freeze-frame photo of inaction and indecision. Eight thousand passengers (many of whom had already spent five or six hours in the air) were literally imprisoned on 30 Northwest flights for as long as eight and a half hours without food, water, or working toilets. One passenger went into diabetic shock. Mothers ran out of formula and diapers for their babies. An irate executive used his cell phone to track down Northwest's CEO (waking him in the middle of the night) to appeal for help. Fights broke out. Passengers threatened to blow open emergency exit doors. Northwest pilots screamed at ground staff over the radio to tow the planes to the gates before they lost all control of the situation.

A congressional investigation, extremely critical reports issued by the Department of Transportation, and four lawsuits all found Northwest Airlines guilty of many acts of omission. By inflexibly adhering to "procedures" for ground operations and "rules" for passenger safety, those in charge overlooked many possible solutions. They could have brought the planes near the gates and let passengers off on the tarmac or they could have disembarked them on the airfield and bused them to the terminal. Alternatively, they could have brought service vehicles out to the planes to deliver food, water, videos, baby formula, and diapers.

The Northwest story is interesting because it lacks any sign of a living system's capacity to self-organize. The principal reason was that the company's traditional style of management had squeezed all intelligence out of the "nodes" that needed to respond in an unscripted manner. Northwest's rigidity proved toxic to intelligent life.

Self-organization was missing that night in Detroit. It would have arisen naturally had employees both understood the larger context and maintained threshold levels of mastery such that Northwest's Operations Center could delegate with confidence that the people below would do the right thing. Imagine what might have been possible if the CEO, instead of hiding behind echelons of flack catchers, had put the word out to all hands: "We have a huge disruption here. I want you all to be as innovative and imaginative as is safely possible to demonstrate to our customers that we can come through when it counts." This would have shifted Northwest from the mode of "listen and comply" to "anticipate and preempt, interpret and improvise." But employees at Northwest Airlines lacked both the context and the mastery to do what was needed.

Ironically, the system behaved like a stereotypical army—unthinking and slavish in its adherence to doctrine and the chain of command. In contrast, the U.S. Army has taken the managerial high ground. Facing conditions infinitely more dangerous and unpredictable than those encountered that night at Detroit Airport, the Army trains soldiers to exploit unforeseen situations for competitive advantage.

Self-organization and emergence are important to many businesses today because they generate undreamed-of paths (new routes) and unimagined places (new destinations). For example, the swelling self-organizing ranks of Linux's independent open systems programmers (now 30 million strong and growing) are continuously identifying new routes as they generate what is becoming the dominant source of global server software. As a result of their self-organizing and self-policing protocols, their applications are immediately exposed to the Darwinian scrutiny of peer review. Software that survives is more robust and suffers from fewer bugs than the commercial server products released by corporations. The Linux Army is also discovering new destinations. An emergent outcome of its newfound prowess is a recent decision to compete with the likes of Microsoft and develop PC applications as well.

New destinations most often arise from unlikely combinations. Nature has demonstrated repeatedly that the most radical possibilities open up when intraspecies cooperation takes place. Within a species, innovation typically fosters new routes. Across species, new destinations often arise from improbable combinations. Some of the most radical innovations in biotechnology are taking place in unlikely crossovers between fish and mammals, fungi and insects, animals and plants. That's why Linux, drawing on such a heterogeneous array of talents and backgrounds, is such a potent force.

The distinction between new routes and new destinations is evident in the earlier Monsanto example. Monsanto's initial focus was on new routes: reinventing agriculture to meet humanity's needs through new genetic routes for disease- and drought-resistant crops. In fitness landscape terms, Monsanto was seeking a route toward a yet-to-be-defined life sciences fitness peak. Monsanto's competitors on this landscape were familiar life sciences companies like DuPont, Zeneca, and Novartis.

Then, as noted, the landscape itself changed as biotechnology in general—and genetically modified crops, in particular— became the target of Greenpeace and environmental groups. In the face of this disruptive shift, Monsanto endured a 20 percent decrease in its market value and was eventually forced to merge with Upjohn to form Pharmacia. But for the better part of a year, Monsanto continued to seek new routes toward its initial destination, blinded by persistence or denial from seeing that the goal posts had been moved (or, arguably, torn down)! In fitness landscape terms, the game had changed. New destinations, not new routes, were called for.

We can only speculate as to what such a new destination might be. One possible scenario could entail Monsanto's shift in focus from global-competitor-and-pioneer-in-the-life-sciences to convener-of-global-conversations-to explore-proper-safeguards-for-bioengineered-crops-and-the-potential-use-of-bioengineered-staples-to-reduce-world-hunger. To be sure, this entails very different skills. But the shift *is* possible.

An extreme interpretation of self-organization and emergence might lead some to turn an organization's members loose and let them self-organize in any way they like. But neither logic nor experience supports such a wholesale abandonment of discipline and structure. Individuals left entirely to their own devices are unlikely to self-organize and generate productive outcomes. China's Cultural Revolution destroyed all that stood out from, or above, the norm. The prolonged upheaval rent the fabric of Chinese society and spiraled toward the lowest common denominators. Reckless and unchanneled self-organization tumbled from the edge into chaos itself and set China back for decades. Productive self-organization requires boundaries.

It is also important to address the opposite extreme, where self-organization is sought and then throttled back through excessive control. The past 30 years' flirtation with "participative management" and "self-managed teams" is a case in point. These constructs rely, to some extent, on self-organization and emergence. But, as with mushrooms, many of which look alike, reports of poisonings remind us that similarities can be dangerously deceptive.

There are six guidelines for harnessing self-organization and emergence:

1. *Decide whether self-organization and emergence are really needed.* Do you face an adaptive challenge? Are new routes or new destinations sought? If nimbleness is required and discontinuous innovation is necessary, these dual properties can add value. Use the right tool for the right task.

2. *Analyze the health of your network.* Self-organization arises from networks that are fueled by nodes and connections. If you seek self-organization, enlarge the number of nodes and expect every organizational member to contribute. Enrich the quality of the connections with simple routines and protocols that cement strong relationships. The U.S. Army has done a great job of this.

3. *Remember the Goldilocks principle: neither too many rules nor too few.* The key to self-organization resides in the tension between discipline and freedom. Nature achieves this tension through selection pressures (which impose discipline) and by upending occurrences (such as chance mutations and environmental disruptions). In organizations, rules provide discipline. They can take the form of protocols: the Army trains soldiers to perform key tasks under a variety of conditions, up to specified standards, and uses After Action Reviews to assess proficiency. Freedom is reinforced by the power of a strange attractor (for example, success against an enemy in the battlefield or the Army's challenge to recruits: "Be All That You Can Be").

4. *Harness the power of Requisite Variety.* Juxtapose people from different fields and backgrounds and let their varied work histories enrich the potential of self-organizing networks. This mixing cannot be done with abandon. But, as is evident in

Silicon Valley, coevolution fosters unlikely forms of cooperation and can open the door to whole new worlds.

5. *Look for the preconditions of emergence:* the existence of "noise" or "heat" in the system; contradictions between words and actions; incongruencies between supply and demand; unexpressed needs. All hint at *emergent* possibilities and help identify when an issue is bubbling toward the surface. "An idea whose time has come" is the conventional way we talk about emergence.

6. *Do not think of self-organization and emergence exclusively as episodic occurrences.* True, self-organization can occur episodically (as it did at Monsanto), and emergence gives rise to periodic upwellings (for example, the emerging global consensus on the inherent dangers of tobacco products). But these properties also have enduring power, as evidenced in Silicon Valley and the U.S. Army. When brought to the forefront of management consciousness, they can become sources of sustaining competitive advantage. They can exert a subtle influence—more akin to the way water wears away stone than to the way dynamite blasts through it.

Federal Express recently discovered the fourth principle—*"You can disturb but never wholly direct a living system"*—the hard way. FedEx management sought to optimize pilot utilization and shave costs off its routing of airplanes. At first blush, it all seemed straightforward. The common denominator, as in many similar situations, is the application of linear logic to a living system. But the fourth principle reminds us that such endeavors almost always backfire.

FedEx's goal (to increase pilot productivity by streamlining aircraft routing) seemed within reach, given more powerful computers and recent breakthroughs in scheduling algorithms. The anticipated savings (in fuel costs and in pilot hours wasted shuttling from one location to another) were estimated in the hundreds of millions. But FedEx made one mistake: the linear game plan evoked a nonlinear response.

The fourth principle of complexity reminds us that we can't *direct* a living system, but FedEx thought it could. Pilots began to complain as the system spit out nightmarish flight plans that required them to blast across the time zones of two hemispheres, with back-to-back transpacific and transatlantic flights, then spend hours in vans and taxis for brief layovers. The *Wall Street Journal*'s Douglas Blackmon reported the complaints as they developed.

As pilot angst mounted, FedEx management stood fast and systems analysts worked around the clock to correct the problems. But redoubled efforts at the wrong thing produce more of the wrong thing. With no relief to the scheduling nightmare in sight, FedEx's 3,500 pilots galvanized into action. They revitalized their traditionally compliant in-house union and threatened a work stoppage if their demands were not met. Their first demand was predictable: "Abandon the new flight-scheduling system!" But self-organization has a way of generating an emergent life of its own. Now mobilized by their protest, the pilots also demanded a 24 percent wage increase over three years, fewer required flying hours per month, and dramatically increased retirement benefits. Confronted with the first pilot strike in the company's history, FedEx management retreated. The optimization model that triggered the uproar was eviscerated, and management acceded to many of the pilots' other requests.

Reflecting on this incident, let us acknowledge that FedEx management began with a reasonable objective; it was its mechanistic routes to implementation that caused all the trouble. Management wished to take the classic "blank sheet of paper" approach and reengineer the inefficient system. The trouble is, the "blank sheet of paper" gets soiled in the execution phase. The fourth principle teaches us that optimization seldom yields radical innovation. At best, it only maximizes the preexisting model. It founders because efforts to direct living systems, beyond very general goals, are counterproductive. Like the proverbial butterfly, living things can be ushered forth with reasonable expectation of progress but they proceed in their own unique way. This seldom conforms to the linear path that we have in mind.

In fitness landscape terms, it is impossible to get to a distant and higher fitness peak (discover radical breakthroughs) by climbing still higher on the peak one is already on (optimizing). Rather, one needs to descend into the unknown, disregard the proven cause-and-effect formulas, and defy the odds. One embarks on a journey of sequential disturbances and adjustments, not a lockstep march along a predetermined path. We may only be able to see as far as our headlights, but proceeding in this fashion can still bring us to our journey's destination.

Because discontinuous leaps, by their very nature, arise from unforeseen combinations, it is impossible to reverse engineer them. Extrapolation is possible when systems exhibit continuity over a wide range of conditions. In this circumstance, the relationship of the components is linear and the goal can be attained by progressing step by step. But if the system exhibits discontinuities, extrapolating "what's going to happen next" is unreliable. Something that does not lend itself to logical explanation after the fact does not respond predictably to direction beforehand. We must settle, instead, for a series of shrewd disruptions, proceeding with a reasonable degree of confidence that the outcome will tilt more in the desired direction than its opposite. When we overreach and attempt to hardwire a specific result, we almost always fail. Nobel Laureate Francis Crick, co-discoverer of the helical structure of DNA, once observed that "Evolution is more clever than you are." What trips us up is our inability to predict second- and third-order consequences that flow from seemingly straightforward intentions. Managers described as "street-smart" or "seasoned" have often garnered this wisdom about living systems the hard way. These veterans expect detailed plans to go awry. They know that the number of things that can go wrong is multiplied when a bold break with the past is attempted. If, in addition, the desired change antagonizes an organization's members (as we saw at FedEx) and they band together to "beat the system," all bets are off. "(N)othing is more difficulty to carry out, nor more doubtful of success, nor more dangerous to handle," observed Machiavelli, "than achieving a new order of things."

At the core of all this unpredictability are two factors. One is the inherently *indeterministic* nature of Nature. Life is shaped by probabilities, not certainties. Parents discover the importance of indeterminism in the unfolding lives of living systems called "children." The second is *frozen accidents*, which occur occasionally and stem from an avalanche of consequences that are difficult to alter. As in a real avalanche, little actions trigger bigger ones that become irreversible. In business, frozen accidents do not obey the laws of scarcity (like diamonds); they follow the laws of plenitude (like language). The more accepted and available something becomes, the faster it accelerates ahead of its rivals and thrives. It becomes "frozen-in" as the de facto standard.

Gary Kildall, someone you've probably never heard of, learned about indeterminism the hard way. The results left an indelible mark on the computer industry. In the early 1960s, Kildall headed one of the few companies that had perfected a clean and efficient operating system for personal computers. He called it CP/M. With the intention of licensing his system, executives of IBM's then-fledgling personal computer unit paid a call on Kildall at his Albuquerque headquarters. The IBM team had previously screened and tested the system and were favorably impressed. But Kildall showed up late and did not display sufficient deference toward the white-shirted executives from Armonk. Returning to the East Coast after a frustrating day, the IBM team pondered its next step in what was obviously going to be an uneasy courtship.

Meanwhile, Bill Gates's mother was on the United Way Board of Directors with IBM CEO John Opel. When she overheard Opel describing the disappointing trip to Albuquerque, she chimed in, saying, "My son, Billy, has built an operating system."

Opel showed more than polite interest. Three weeks later, IBM visited Gates to examine what he jokingly called his "Dirty Old Operating System"—DOS for short. A month later IBM made an offer; Gates accepted. His net worth is now upward of $40 billion. In 1994, Kildall—bitter and disillusioned—died in a bikers' bar in Monterey, California.

Viewed through the lens of the fourth principle of complexity, unforeseen consequences in this case flowed from, first, Kildall's tardiness and his seeming indifference toward the IBM team; next, a chance encounter between Bill Gates's mother and the IBM CEO; and finally, the commercial leverage bequeathed to DOS once it was embedded in IBM PCs. Some of this sequence might have been anticipated; most of it came as a surprise. Microsoft was swept into the mainstream of the information industry with astonishing velocity. As economist Brian Arthur observes, "Microsoft's success is clever strategy, mediocre technology and a hell of a lot of indeterminism, and increasing returns."

Frozen accidents are coincidences that become locked in. *Indeterminism* deals the cards. Frozen accidents are what happen at the gaming table after the cards are dealt. Frozen accidents are the means by which a species acquires its destiny. Once a cell in an embryo embarks on a particular pathway, it leaves behind many other options. The number of cells it can change into from that point forward greatly diminishes. When a niche is wide open, one sees many prototypes. But as the niche is filled, extremes are weeded out. One sees this in e-commerce today.

So are there guidelines that can help us disturb things in the general direction we'd like them to go? Ancient masters of the Eastern martial arts had insight into how one co-opts the energy of a living system long before there were institutes in Santa Fe. *Jujitsu* means the gentle way. *Karate* means the empty hand. Both images seem counterintuitive when confronted with an opponent hell-bent on doing harm. Both rely on deflecting or harnessing an opposing force or energy toward desired goals—a concept FedEx roundly ignored.

At the more concrete level of corporate application, there are three general guidelines:

- Design, don't engineer.
- Discover, don't dictate.
- Decipher, don't presuppose.

Consider airports in this context. The lounge areas surrounding each gate do not have signs or attendants who tell us not to talk too loudly, occupy more than one seat, or block the aisles. Yet, through the invisible hand of design, all these objectives are broadly accomplished. Seats are arranged so that conversation takes place with those in the immediate vicinity and not with those far away. Fixed armrests between seats prevent people from lying down and occupying seats that others may need. Seats are bolted together in rows, making movement of furniture difficult. Thus passengers are discouraged from rearranging the floor plan, blocking aisles, or inconveniencing the cleaning staff that comes late at night. The remarkable quality of design is that it seems to just happen; it works its magic without our awareness of how it does so. From the architect's perspective, what we are experiencing is an evolved discipline of disturbing, not directing, a living system at work.

In contrast, the rock that traditional management founders on is its obsession with directing the insurgent nature of social systems and their capacity, in turn, to subvert programmed change. A 1995 *Fortune* article, "Making Change Stick," addressed the difficulty and opened with a series of quotations resonating with the experience of many. In that article, MIT professor-turned-consultant Michael Hammer (coauthor of *Reengineering the Corporation*) explained the source of all the difficulty:

> Human beings' innate resistance to change is the most perplexing, annoying, distressing and confusing part of reengineering. [But] resistance to change is natural and inevitable. To think that resistance won't occur, to view those who exhibit its symptoms as difficult or intractable, is a fatal mistake. The real cause of reengineering failure is not the resistance itself, but management's failure to deal with it. Most dissenters won't stand and shout at you that they hate what you're doing to them and their comfortable old ways. Instead, they will nod, smile and agree with everything you say—and they behave as they always have. This is the kiss of 'yes.'

Not so fast. What we've been saying about living systems offers a different perspective. That these comments resonate with many people's change experience may suggest that we have been working against, rather than flowing with, the nature of things. The explanations offered may say more about the backlash directed at trying to hardwire behavior than about any valid evidence of innate human resistance to change.

A contrasting version of the earlier example of an airport lounge makes the point. In the former Soviet Union, some airports equipped their waiting areas with folding chairs. These were arranged in rows, and signs and announcements broadcast stern admonitions not to move the chairs, block aisles, and so forth. Security personnel occasionally enforced these policies, but passengers moved the chairs anyway to accommodate clusters of friends. The armless chairs were redeployed as beds or rearranged to make surfaces for dining or for playing cards. Children built ingenious play structures. And custodians complained of the extra work of restoring the rows before cleaning.

One way of thinking would identify all this as the predictable fallout from trying to overcontrol living things. Passengers had to be controlled to compensate for design shortcomings. In contrast, the airport lounge in the earlier example achieves the desired behavior with no overt rules or commands. With the right design, people can be people without compromising the purposes of the space.

When change is driven from above and moves along a predetermined path, or when members of living systems are marched lockstep in frontal assaults on the fortress of discontinuous change, their efforts almost always fail. But if we *design* (and don't engineer), *discover* what's working and build on that (and don't dictate), and then *decipher* the second- and third-order consequences (rather than presuppose that it will all work as programmed) we are far more likely to succeed. When properly mobilized, the so-called resistant masses or "permafrost of middle management" simply cease to exist as such.

Richard Tanner Pascale is a leading business consultant worldwide, a best-selling author, and a respected scholar. This article is based on ideas drawn from *Surfing the Edge of Chaos*, coauthored with Mark Millemann and Linda Gioja.

7

Better Than Plan

Managing Beyond the Budget

Douglas K. Smith

Typical annual planning and budgeting falls short for three reasons. First, it fails to specify outcome-based goals rather than activity-based goals, which make outcomes difficult to measure. Second, it fails to measure success directly against key performance challenges. Third, it fails to inspire people to excel. The people responsible for each performance challenge should be grouped in a way that makes sense and charged with setting and achieving outcome-based goals, which can be measured against the organization's mission. Planning and budgeting must become part of a performance-outcomes (rather than functional) management system.

Annual planning and budgeting processes are the most formalized, drawn out, and resource-intensive goal-setting efforts in organizations today. Indeed, with the sometime exception of personal development plans, budgeting and planning are the *only* organization-wide goal-setting effort in many companies. Yet, notwithstanding their high profile and reputed importance, they are often pointless exercises. Consider the following tale.

One day in June, Mary, the operations chief for GrandVision, met the CEO to discuss the next year's annual plan and budget. The CEO had spoken to analysts in May and painted a bright future of double-digit growth in revenues and profits. "Now, we must deliver," the CEO told Mary. "For GrandVision to succeed, you will have to be aggressive with head count and costs. We all have to aim high!"

Mary spent most of June with her finance VP figuring out just how much head count and expense she could load into her budget and still be considered a team player by the CEO and a heroine when her numbers came in better than plan. Mary did want to aim high—just not too high. She wasn't being cynical; for operations to contribute to the CEO's many strategic initiatives—quality improvement, speed, reengineering, technology-based innovation, and strategic alliances—she needed people and budget.

In July she asked a direct report into her office. "Dick," she said earnestly, "this year we must be aggressive with head count and expenses. What can you do to help?" The next day Dick invited his direct report Tom to lunch. Dick repeated Mary's exhortations. Because there were only eight people in his department and little nonpersonnel-related expenses, Tom didn't have much room to maneuver. He spent most of August working the numbers with his people. They spoke often about quality, speed, reengineering, and the other challenges they faced, but gave little thought to how to measure success against those challenges. Instead, they focused on the numbers.

Over the next month, Tom, Dick, and Mary presented their initial plans to their respective bosses; each knew the numbers would be rejected but viewed their proposals as an opening gambit. Each was told to go back with a sharper pencil.

Throughout October and November and on into December, Tom, Dick, and Mary retraced the ground already covered in June, July, August, and September. Each asked the next to aim high while personally aiming low but not too low because each wanted to appear to be aiming high—at least high enough. Lots of pencils got sharpened.

Everyone spoke fervently about the strategic initiatives ahead. But as the days grew shorter, Tom, Dick, and Mary worked harder and harder at the one objective all knew was top priority: submitting an annual plan and budget by mid-December that contained the right and best numbers.

And they did! The executives headed home for the holidays with relief. Each returned in January ready to focus on quality improvement, speed, reengineering, technology-based innovation, and strategic alliances. They had no goals to direct their efforts, but they knew the activities were important and budgeted for.

One cold morning shortly after returning to work, Mary was planning a meeting for January 15th on "Stepping Up to This Year's Challenges" when the phone rang. It was the CFO. "Mary," he groaned, "I've got bad news."

"Oh, no," cried Mary. "Not the budget?"

"No, the budget is fine. We need to go over last year's numbers. If we're going to meet the analysts' expectations, we have to take down some reserves in operations. Can you clear your calendar for the 15th?"

Financial Fictions

A fable? Not really. This story may simplify months of pointless activity. But it does not misrepresent them. The exercise in numerology that we call "annual planning and budgeting" does not occur just "once upon a time." It happens every year in every organization of any significant size and scope. Despite the time and effort we invest, this process falls short for at least three reasons:

1. *It fails to specify outcomes instead of activities.* Performance begins with a focus on outcome-based goals, not activity-based goals. *Outcome-based goals* describe the results or impacts that directly answer the question "How would you know you succeeded at X?"

For example, if you must improve customer service, then goals should describe outcomes in terms of speed, correct information, lack of errors, customer satisfaction, customer repurchases, and the like. By contrast, *activity-based goals* only restate the activities people plan to do. For customer service, activity-based goals might be "improve customer service," "organize customer service representatives into teams," "train customer service representatives in how to handle upset customers," and "install new automated response system." Each of these *might* produce outcomes; each *might* be important to do. But activities, however significant, ought not to be goals. *Goals should be the outcomes we hope to achieve as a result of the activities we undertake.*

Effective goals are SMART—specific, measurable, aggressive, relevant, and time-bound (see "The Five Elements of SMART Goals"). If financial yardsticks are the relevant metric for success, use them. But if time, speed, specifications, expectations, satisfaction, quality, new products, new services, trust-based relationships, or any other metric better describes success, use that metric and not revenues, expenses, or head count as the basis for SMART outcome goals.

    2. It fails to measure success directly against key performance challenges. The CEO of GrandVision promised analysts "double-digit growth in revenue and profits." How was GrandVision

---

The Five Elements
of SMART Goals

To truly measure and sustain success, leaders must focus on *outcomes* that are meaningful to the customer, not on activities that merely occupy an organization. It is important, therefore, to set appropriate performance goals. Effective goals are:

- *Specific.* In specifying performance improvement, for instance, they answer such questions as "at what?" "by whom?" and "by how much?"

- *Measurable.* Effective goals can be assessed by a combination of four yardsticks: speed or time; cost; quality or customer expectations; and positive yield, or the impact you hope to deliver for customers, shareholders, or the organization.

- *Aggressive (yet achievable).* Aggressive goals must stretch and inspire us. But to sustain their efforts, people need to feel confident that their goals can actually be accomplished.

- *Relevant.* Goals should pertain directly to the performance challenge you face. They should address the needs of the customer, not the processes of the organization.

- *Time-bound.* Goals must answer the question, "by when?" and must be free of arbitrary constraints (such as the quarter, fiscal year, or academic year) imposed by the organizational calendar.

going to succeed? Through tackling such *performance challenges* as quality improvement, speed, reengineering, technology-based innovation, and strategic alliances. For most of these, however, revenue, expense, and head count are lagging and indirect indicators of success. And, because financial results lag everything an organization does, financial results often fail to explain the success or failure of any single thing an organization does. Tom, Dick, and Mary could meet their head count and expense goals and still have no idea whether quality improvement, speed, reengineering, technology-based innovation, and strategic alliances had made any difference. To track success at each of these challenges, Tom, Dick, and Mary would need to use metrics and goals that were relevant to the challenges themselves.

3. *It fails to inspire people to excel.* Goals should excite as well as reward. But few people come to work thrilled by the challenge of meeting head count and expense targets. By contrast, when people set goals to shorten cycle times, dramatically reduce customer-defined defects, establish new service levels, or go after new customers or markets, their energy, focus, and sense of achievement all rise.

To be sure, organizations must be disciplined about choosing among too many opportunities in the face of too few resources. As Herbert Simon noted in his 1945 classic *Administrative Behavior*, budgetary and planning processes can help build this discipline: "The budget, first of all, forces a simultaneous consideration of all the competing claims for support. Second, the budget transports upward in the administrative hierarchy the decisions as to fund allocation to a point where competing values must be weighed, and where functional (self-interest) will not lead to a faulty weighting of values."

As we move into the 21st century, however, Simon's logic has crumbled under the weight of three realities that leaders must now confront:

1. *Dollars are no longer the sole nor the best criterion for selecting among competing performance challenges.* Financial results still measure the performance *of the business as a whole*. But they often fail to measure success against specific performance challenges such as speed, quality, customer satisfaction, reengineering, continuous improvement, innovation, diversity, partnering, alliances, and so on. Time, talent, quality, and relationships are as critical as money in evaluating the benefits and costs associated with such performance challenges.

In a world like Simon's, where executive choice was limited to putting a scarce dollar into sales versus operations, valuing the return on that dollar in terms of operational efficiencies versus sales growth was straightforward. A dollar in sales got so many dollars of sales growth. A dollar in operations got so many dollars of efficiencies. Which dollars of benefit did the executives want more?

The cost/benefit ratio of reducing the cycle time of order generation through fulfillment might involve dollars, talent, time, defects, relationships, customer satisfaction and loyalty, and learning. Attempting to reduce these *different yardsticks* to dollars only confounds communication and decision making. When it comes time in Simon's logic for executives to compare costs and benefits across differing performance challenges (say, reengineering versus quality versus strategic alliances), the executives discuss and debate their choices in terms of highly theoretical and abstract "dollar equivalents" of impact. It all becomes nonsensical.

2. *The sum of functional performance rarely explains total organization performance.* Annual planning and budgeting, as practiced by organizations, assumes a purely functional, pyramidal view of organization structure and performance. Yet every organization I know faces serious performance challenges that demand cross-functional and even cross-company coordination. Designating responsibilities for such challenges in the straitjacket of functional, budgetary buckets may gratify finance professionals. But such allocations have little to do with setting, monitoring, or achieving outcome-based goals against the relevant performance challenges themselves.

3. *Market requirements seldom conform to the cycle of annual budgets.* In annual planning and budgeting, all effort and results are monitored by the month, quarter, and year. But today's performance challenges have their own internal clocks for success. Few of us still rely on phases of the moon to plan our personal and professional lives. Why, then, do we persist in assessing progress against quality, strategic alliance building, and other performance challenges in terms of months, quarters, and years? Is it administratively convenient? Yes, for the administrators. But it is neither convenient nor constructive for people trying to measure and deliver success.

Not-So-Hidden Costs

Leaders ignore these new realities at their peril. Persisting in traditional planning and budgeting processes creates serious shortcomings:

Poor choices are poorly made. Ambiguity and turf politics combine to drive out rationality in choosing which performance challenges to tackle. Is it credible for GrandVision to simultaneously pursue quality improvement, speed, reengineering, technology-based innovation, and strategic alliances? Maybe. But if a choice had to be made, how could that choice be rational in the absence of clearly defined outcomes regarding speed, expectations, loyalty, satisfaction, skills, and values? It cannot. Decisions and debates over revenue, cost, and head count only generate ambiguity and confusion—and lead to destructive politicking rather than collaborative decision making.

Activity-based goals proliferate instead of outcome-based goals. Consider again Tom, Dick, and Mary. When they returned in January, they had plenty of activity-based goals. They would "train people in quality," "increase speed," "reengineer core processes," and "build strategic alliances"—all within budgeted expense and head count levels. But these goals only restate activities. Activity-based goals are self-fulfilling. We say we will build, or train, or coordinate, or implement. When asked, "Have you done so?" we say yes—and point to the activities themselves.

Organizations across the globe are strewn with the wreckage of speed, quality, teaming, reengineering, partnering, and other strategic initiatives that seemingly ask people to commit to a bunch of activities—change for its own sake—instead of demanding that they set and achieve outcome-based performance goals that matter.

Opportunity to build skills and behaviors is lost. In today's opportunity-rich, talent-starved organizations, every business process should build needed skills and behaviors. In theory, budgeting and planning processes could produce many new skills and behaviors, including mastery of outcome-based performance metrics and goals. In practice, however, annual budgeting and planning processes succeed only in amplifying negotiating skills and cynical behaviors.

Doing Performance Planning Right

Jennifer Dunlap, as vice president of the American Red Cross, decided to enrich her budgeting process with an outcomes focus. As head of Corporate Services, responsible for human resources, marketing, communications, fundraising events, governmental relations, and international services, she asked her staff to prepare their usual budgets for the coming year—but these budgets would simply provide a necessary appendix. She wanted the body of her plan to focus on the key performance challenges identified by leaders of Corporate Services as well as the outcome-based goals critical to succeeding at those challenges.

For each performance challenge, she asked leaders to specify one or more outcome-based goals as well as the major activities needed to achieve those goals. For example, she knew that marketing needed to build strategic partnerships with corporations. But instead of focusing on the budget and head count required, she wanted marketing to articulate one or more outcome-based goals regarding the number of and timing with which such partnerships would be established as well as the specific impacts each partnership would have.

In addition, instead of shoehorning their goals and reviews into months, quarters, and year-end, people were asked to designate review points appropriate to the time frames for success. And they were to indicate how each performance challenge supported the mission of the organization.

Dunlap reminded everyone that Corporate Services and the larger organization confronted many more opportunities and performance challenges than they had resources to tackle. Choices would be made. But she insisted that they choose by comparing relevant outcomes, such as speed, skills, talents, quality, donor and alliance relationships, and retention *as well as* dollars of donor contributions and expenses.

Instead of the drudgery and anxiety of budget discussions, people worked hard to understand and articulate the outcomes they hoped to produce and why those outcomes mattered to the beneficiaries, customers, staff, and donors. Many Corporate Service leaders realized they had to spend time talking with the people who had firsthand experience with key constituents. They discovered many performance challenges that demanded coordination across departments within their division as well as the organization. This, in turn, induced leaders to seek commitments to outcome-based goals from people beyond their own departments. It produced a more integrated set of challenges that would demand teamwork within Corporate Services instead of perpetuating the department-by-department view of work promoted by traditional planning and budgeting.

Did Corporate Services produce and submit a budget? Yes. But managers spent most of their planning and budgeting time doing something far more important—identifying and agreeing on the key performance challenges and outcome-based goals by which they could make the biggest difference to the beneficiaries, customers, donors, and staff of the organization.

Getting Started

How can leaders tame the budget and planning beast? First, stop the charade. Make planning and budgeting just one part of a performance outcomes management system that, at any moment and every moment, shows a complete picture of the performance challenges being pursued by your organization; the outcome-based goals that measure success against those challenges; the time frames within which that success is expected; and the people (individually and in combinations) responsible for and committed to those outcomes.

To implement this system, you and your colleagues must take several concrete steps:

View performance challenges, not departments and functions, as the focal point for planning and goal setting. Instead of positioning function and business budgets as the centerpiece, use the performance challenges themselves. For example, GrandVision ought to construct a plan that directly treats quality improvement, speed, reengineering, technology-based innovation, and strategic alliances. Should there be a budget for operations? Yes. But it should only be considered, reviewed, and updated when operational expense and head count matter to the performance challenge at hand.

Group the people responsible for each performance challenge in ways that make sense, and demand that they set and achieve outcome-based goals. Every organization comprises many "working arenas"—the venues in which performance occurs. For many decades, performance always happened in simple, self-contained places: individual jobs, departments, divisions. Today performance usually occurs in much more complex and ephemeral settings: project teams, business processes, strategic alliances.

Different working arenas are relevant to different performance challenges. But every such challenge and its relevant set of working arenas ought to have SMART goals and metrics. Planning, budgeting, and review processes ought to help people ask and answer the following questions:

What is the performance challenge at hand?

What outcomes would indicate success at this challenge?

What are the working arenas and people necessary to this challenge?

To which of those working arenas do I or we contribute?

What outcome-based goals should we set and pursue to make that contribution?

Make trade-off decisions on the basis of all the relevant metrics for anticipated costs and benefits. Instead of perpetuating the fiction that all corporate actions can be converted into their "dollar impacts," leaders must gain confidence and skill at debating performance alternatives (quality improvement, speed, and so on) in the very terms that measure success for those alternatives. By doing so, they can lead themselves and others to get increasingly good at articulating and achieving outcome-based goals.

Annual planning and budgeting processes, however well intended, have mutated into mathematical and political exercises with little relevance to performance. Instead of making success measurable, they generate activity-based goals and cynical negotiating skills. Most companies could scrap the entire process, ask the finance function to provide the needed picture of costs and revenues, and do better in terms of overall business performance. Better still, every organization I know could implement a performance outcomes measurement system and provide superior, sustainable value to customers, shareholders or donors, and the people of the enterprise. By doing so, organizations would perform much "better than plan."

Douglas K. Smith is a consultant specializing in organization performance, innovation, and change. Named in *The Guru Guide* as one of the world's leading management thinkers, he is author or coauthor of five books, including *Make Success Measurable*. His work has been featured in *BusinessWeek*, the *Wall Street Journal*, the *Harvard Business Review*, the *New York Times*, and the *McKinsey Quarterly*.

8

An Alternative to Hierarchy

Gifford Pinchot

In contrast to hierarchical systems, the basis for most knowledge-work relationships is the defining principle of community: generosity. Egalitarian members gain status by giving away valuable resources. People help one another across boundaries because they share a common purpose. People have the latitude to make decisions and the incentives to innovate and to deliver more and better services for less money, faster. They can help one another to correct breakdowns in the system. Intrapreneurial teams can think strategically about their services because they know where their customers are heading. They are empowered and motivated.

Creating community is an essential leadership skill. As hierarchical organizations based on dominance and submission prove less and less suited to the times, effective leaders are reinventing the workplace as a community based on fellowship and service. Leaders, after all, cannot order commitment, innovation, and energy from unwilling followers. Commitment, innovation, and energy—and the willingness to cooperate across boundaries—grow only in a healthy community of work.

Of course, few organizations exist as pure hierarchies or pure communities; every organization, like every human being, has the capacity for both selfish pursuit and altruistic service. But in the Information Age, the rapid spread of knowledge and the heightened need for fluid patterns of cooperation are bringing community to the forefront, both in the workplace and in the wider society.

Today's workers frequently need to gather and to apply knowledge across the boundaries of the organization. They do so by creating informal networks. From the biases of Western economics, these informal networkers are seen as exchanging favors—helping each other out because they know that someday they will need favors in return. From the viewpoint of community, however, the behaviors of the network are better understood as manifestations of the *gift economy*—one of the six leadership keys to building community.

Building the Gift Economy

The gift economy is built on the defining principle of community—generosity. It is also the basis for most knowledge-work relationships. In a traditional community or in a knowledge community members gain status by giving away rather than keeping valuable resources. Defining success by what one gives away rather than what one has is neither a new practice nor an overly idealistic view of human motivation. It is deeply rooted in the human psyche, in history, and in everyday life. Science, for instance, works on the principle of the gift economy. You *give* a paper. How much knowledge you have means little in the academic world; how much you have contributed to your field means everything. A person who adds new knowledge is honored—one who simply knows everything in the field is third rate.

In knowledge organizations, the workings of the gift economy resemble the pattern we might have seen in a small village in 1750. Imagine a skilled blacksmith who can create more value than he needs for his own family. This leaves time and energy free, which the blacksmith uses to help raise a neighbor's barn or fix a hoe for a needy neighbor. In this village, although the free market provides a structure of exchange, marketplace success by itself doesn't confer high status. Social position depends on being good enough in the marketplace to have not just a fine Sunday suit or a nice house but also the time, skills, and resources to make gifts of service to others in the community. When serving the larger good is chosen freely, community flourishes.

People help each other across the boundaries of the best Information Age organizations because they share common purposes. Their status in the informal organization is largely based on their expertise and the degree to which they share it with others. There is, to be sure, an element of central governance. But innovation comes from a combination of generous collaboration and a feedback and control process that I call *free intraprise*—an internal market that gives buyers and sellers of internal services a choice of providers and of customers.

Bureaucracy by its nature inhibits collaboration across boundaries. To our surprise, freer, more market-oriented systems like the village of 1750 provide a firmer base for community spirit and cross-boundary generosity than any bureaucracy can.

In large organizations, the work most people do can be seen as a service to others within the organization. Market researchers provide information to product managers; maintenance workers provide services to the manufacturing function. Increasingly, large organizations in all sectors of the economy are letting people with better, faster, and cheaper ways of providing those services sell them across the boundaries of the organization. For example, Dave Steinke, in the Rocky Mountain Region of the U.S. Forest Service, not only makes videos for his own region but also makes and sells them to other regions as well. The result is both better service to the Eastern Region and lower cost for his own region.

Creating Internal Markets

Like hierarchy and community, internal market competition can be a powerful ordering principle, building on what works best and eliminating less effective ways of working. Just as free enterprise can release the energy of an economy burdened with totalitarian control, free intraprise is the antidote to command-and-control organization of corporations and government agencies in the democratic West. But competition can take two forms. One form of competition gives buyers choice and sellers an opportunity to become the provider of choice for their clients or coworkers. That produces a powerful incentive to figure out how to deliver more service for less money, faster.

The other form leads people to look upward to the boss to curry favor and thus to be awarded a larger monopoly of power. The first brings out the desire to serve; the second brings out the desire to politic, position, and point fingers.

Organizations that rely only on the chain of command encourage the unproductive, self-serving kind of competition. People in very hierarchical organizations almost inevitably struggle for the favor of those in power; those in cooperative networks look not to their boss, but to themselves, their colleagues, and ultimately their customers for feedback. It is the marketplace that provides the ultimate feedback on performance. It allows a contribution to be measured and rewarded based on what you do for the users, not what you do for the hierarchy.

To encourage productive competition and innovation, companies such as Hewlett-Packard, 3M, and Du Pont are beginning to free their staff service providers from the control of a particular business unit, and are giving their business units the choice of service provider, whether in-house or outside. Having more than one place to go in the company for, say, marketing or software engineering services seems like it would lead to chaos. But experience suggests the opposite: when you introduce choice, you get more accurate feedback and higher quality. The quality movement itself grew because customers could exercise choice and demanded more. A monopoly doing a customer survey to find out whether it is providing good customer service—and promising to do better if the answer is no—is not enough to cause change. The results can always be rationalized if customers have no choice. To radically reorient a business around the needs of customers, leaders must hear, "I won't be using your services anymore because another provider is serving me better."

This kind of immediate, unambiguous, and sometimes painful feedback is what people respond to. It gives internal customers throughout the organization a measure of power through their ability to choose a provider. The business units get better service because the intrapreneurs providing services are motivated to innovate. As a result, staff monopolies are no longer protected from external or internal groups offering better service at a better price. Technologies and better ways of doing things spread faster.

Community service and competition need not be antagonists. With effective leadership, everyone balances the need to win as a work group or department with the larger need to win as an organization. The problem in a chain-of-command organization is the lack of objective standards of performance. Managers tend to "raise the bar" on the performance of each subunit until managers and employees alike have little left to give beyond what is demanded by their bosses. That feeds a selfish turf mentality.

Through personal inspiration or exhortation, many leaders seek to add a spirit of community—they usually call it *teamwork*—to a basically bureaucratic system of control. This can work in small or narrowly focused organizations but grows increasingly difficult as size and complexity increase. A robust community calls for genuine commitment and radical change. Giving people the latitude to make sound business decisions—and giving them a real stake in the success of their group—creates the incentives to innovate, improve, and achieve meaningful results. The internal market provides honest feedback. Efficiency and skill are rewarded financially, but, as with the village blacksmith, the sign of true success becomes the ability to create enough value that one can make gifts of time and effort to others in the organization.

Thinking Small

Successful community building often hinges on a basic question—how to balance the needs of the team, the department, or the division with those of the larger enterprise. People tend naturally to affiliate in smaller entities and to commit to those communities in which they can exert a measure of control. The challenge for leaders at all levels is to build commitment both to the smaller team and to the larger whole.

Everybody wants to be engaged in something that is deeply meaningful. Even in small organizations, we tend to form

Creating an Organizational Community

Organizations that distinguish themselves in the marketplace may, on paper, resemble many other enterprises. But in practice, they share the key characteristics and internal cohesion of healthy communities. There are six steps to building a sense of community:

1. *Creating a common purpose.* A worthwhile common purpose contributes to group success. Some organizations focus on a common enemy. It is better to focus on contribution to society. Steve Jobs inspired the highly dedicated culture of Apple's glory days by building "insanely great products" that could liberate people's creative energy and transform society.

2. *Supporting the gift economy.* At Sun Microsystems, each person has an *avatar* (a sort of personal icon) that represents them graphically on the companywide computer system. As a person gives information, renders assistance, and receives praise across the boundaries of Sun, his or her avatar is programmed to acquire hats, clothing, size, and other signs of higher status. Thus Sun has taken the basic logic of community, that one's status rises with giving, and built it into its internal communication system.

3. *Establishing a shared environment.* A common environment—physical and emotional—is a foundation of community. Employee stock ownership and profit sharing plans can increase community spirit because everyone's shares rise and fall together. Sharing financial results weekly lets employees see how the company is doing. Real-time production statistics on electronic readouts at Toyota make contributions visible. The more everyone can see the consequences of each other's work, the more community naturally evolves.

(*continued on next page*)

4. *Moving toward equality*. Huge differences in status based on rank or wealth work against community. The Hewlett-Packard ideal of "an egalitarian workplace where ideas come before hierarchy" defines the best elements of Silicon Valley culture. Information Age organizations everywhere have discovered that removing symbols and perks of rank increases the strength of the organizational community. Eliminate executive parking places and executive dining rooms, and work to open the organization to everyone's voice and best contributions.

5. *Internal not-for-profits*. In any society, the not-for-profit sector helps realize many community goals. In large organizations, support activities that serve the whole tend to be organized as staff groups reporting to powerful executives. However, at Du Pont, for instance, a worthy internal development is supported by "tin cupping"—several business units and staff groups give a bit of their budgets to support a project. This is a rudimentary not-for-profit form inside an organization. Such approaches move projects beneficial to the whole away from centrally allocated budgets to budgets supported by local unit contributions.

6. *Providing safety, security, and love*. A foundation of the community ethic is caring for all its members. Organizations seeking to build community provide a safety net for those who become redundant in part of the enterprise. 3M gives redundant middle managers up to a year on special assignment to find a new job within 3M. The company provides training and help with finding work in another division or function. At its highest level, the community cares for and in essence loves the individual. And the individual, in return, loves the community.

subgroups that see themselves as special, and being part of a special group leads us to make greater sacrifices, work together more smoothly, and focus on the output of the team. Ideally, we would be able to identify ourselves as special at the team level, at the organizational level, at the state level, at the national level, at the world level. But the human soul is not always strong enough to do that without help.

A great test of leadership is creating a strong sense of team specialness that honors people's need to belong to a team while also supporting other parts of the organization. One of the failures of the American management style is the tendency, when something goes wrong, to seek blame. That automatically causes people to defend their own turf against others. By contrast, leaders who view their organization as a total system and a working community can help members correct breakdowns in the system, rather than shifting blame to others.

Fostering Strategic Thinking

Leaders of the organization must define a common destination and a clear strategy. But they must also create space for small intrapreneurial teams to think strategically about the service they are providing. A team serving several divisions within a company needs the space to say, "I see where the medical division is going; I see where the consumer division is going. What training or other changes will it take for us to provide the services they will need three years from now?" In an intelligent organization people at relatively low levels ask such questions because their future depends upon it. And they know that the only way to answer that question is to understand where their customers are heading.

In a large hierarchical organization, most people simply do what they're told and leave thinking about the future to their higher-ups. They have little discretion and therefore little incentive to think about the bigger picture. The leader of a rigid hierarchy, even the leader who excels at defining strategy and direction, will have a hard time implementing a new vision because it takes far longer to translate vision into orders than to motivate empowered employees. When you deny people the opportunity to control their own destiny, you deprive them of the ability to act strategically. Accountable, high-performing individuals and teams have to think strategically about their place in the organization's future. Teams in a free intraprise system control their own futures and reap the results of their decisions, both good and bad. When we combine the feedback of a free intraprise system with a powerful spirit of organizational community, we achieve levels of organizational intelligence that no hierarchy-obsessed corporation can match. To be sure, that begins with a clearly defined, enterprise-wide strategy. But it also requires an organization that lets people engage in such thinking and then act on their conclusions.

Today's workplace is the engine of society. It is also the place where most of us spend most of our time—often at the expense of our families or civic communities. A healthy work community is key to professional happiness, to organizational loyalty, and to the level of cooperation across boundaries that is essential in the Information Age. Creating community requires a deep change of heart and of values. The change is difficult, but no organization can fully engage the energy, creativity, and commitment of knowledge workers unless it first succeeds as a community.

Gifford Pinchot is an author, speaker, and consultant on innovation management. His books, *The End of Bureaucracy and the Rise of the Intelligent Organization* and the best-selling *Intrapreneuring*, have influenced the business and organizational practices of leading corporations, nonprofits, and government agencies.

9

A Passion for the Business

An Interview with Jacques Nasser

It takes work for a large organization to retain passion, agility, urgency, energy, and the ability to act quickly. A leader needs to create an environment in which those with passion for the business, entrepreneurial spirit, and skill are given opportunities to contribute and grow. Organizations must act quickly to respond to long-term social and economic forces. They must embrace change, including change in fundamental assumptions and values. Strategic information and imperatives must be communicated throughout the business to create alignment and an environment that gives people autonomy to determine how best to meet business goals.

Building large organizations that retain the entrepreneurial spirit of small start-up businesses is a challenge facing many leaders. Ford Motor Company has a history of organizational innovation, including work in labor-management partnerships, empowered work teams, and employee involvement. The company, with operations in every region of the world, launched a major change initiative several years ago that consolidated four regional units into integrated global groups for developing, manufacturing, and marketing its products.

Jacques Nasser gained international prominence when he became president and chief executive officer of Ford. Nasser, born in Lebanon, raised in Australia, and fluent in five languages, has worked in a variety of assignments throughout Asia, Europe, and the Americas. He was a key architect of Ford's business revitalization, resulting in record revenues, profits, and shareholder returns. Management consultant Robert Shaw spoke with Nasser about the demands of leadership in a rapidly changing industry.

Robert Shaw: You are sometimes described as an impatient entrepreneur. Passion is a central theme in your business philosophy. How does this work in a corporation as large as Ford?

Jacques Nasser: Passion creates the energy and drive required for any firm to grow. You must, of course, love your product and take pride in delighting customers. My definition of passion, however, goes further. Having a passion for the *business* means that you enjoy balancing the many demands you face. For instance, how do you build the best possible car or truck at the lowest possible cost? Focusing only on a product's features is as inadequate as focusing only on its cost. These are the challenges that make our jobs interesting and require us to be creative as leaders.

RS: Does your passion for the business have a downside? Can people misinterpret your leadership style?

JN: I expect a great deal. How do we drive new growth? How do we improve our efficiencies every year? How do we deepen customer loyalty? In an industry as competitive as ours, you must improve and you must do it fast. I want people to focus on high-leverage areas and fully dedicate themselves to making us stronger as a company. I realize that being part of my team can feel all-consuming. I must say, however, that the passion I feel for the business can never be forced upon people. They feel it or they don't. My job is to create an environment in which those with passion and skill are given every opportunity to contribute to the business and to grow as leaders.

RS: Many of Ford's employees still view the firm as a family business. What does it mean to be a family firm of 360,000 people in a highly competitive industry?

JN: We want the nimbleness, urgency, and energy found in effective family firms. If you are losing money in a family business, you act quickly. You don't sit around and study a problem for six months. You move quickly, act boldly, because the well-being of the enterprise and the family is at stake. A family firm is one in which employees are striving to achieve objectives that will benefit everyone in this generation and in future generations.

In a successful company, there is an emotional feeling that "we are all running the business together." One way of building that sense of affinity is to give people diverse field assignments, where they can experience the power of a small team of people working together to create a successful enterprise. In our more remote operating units, for example, you can't afford the luxury of specialization. These units have the feel of small, entrepreneurial family-run businesses. On a broader scale, employee stock ownership also helps create a shared sense of partnership and clear purpose. Today, over 20 percent of Ford's stock is owned by our employees.

RS: You believe that everything you do as a leader is people related. Yet you are known as a relentless advocate of creating shareholder value and will make tough decisions to enhance your firm's competitiveness. How do you balance these sides of your character?

JN: I have a reputation of being efficiency driven. I don't think it is fair for customers to pay for an organization's inefficiency. It's just wrong to pass the cost of waste on to customers. It's equally wrong to punish shareholders with lower returns, which is inevitable when a firm fails to be competitive. From a larger perspective, you grow as a firm only if you create customer and shareholder value faster than your competition. Remember that our founder created the modern automotive industry with innovations such as mass production that cut the cost of an automobile by two-thirds. Henry Ford was a visionary because he understood that finding innovative ways to maximize customer value was the pathway to growth.

Our goal is not simply to make this year's targets through cost reductions. Our goal is to position us to grow far into the future. In that respect, I am serious about business results and serious about our culture. In today's market, leaders need a variety of skills and capabilities to build an organization that will last. Those who focus only on cost will fail as surely as those who lose sight of it.

RS: You have said that "Nowhere do the winds of change blow as hard as they do in the automotive industry." How do you view the changes in your industry, and what do they suggest for leaders of other organizations?

JN: Most people are inward focused when considering change. You need to examine the broader external context that drives change. An industry as large as the automotive industry is affected by what's going on in the global economy, as well as long-term social and demographic trends, environmental changes, and new technologies. You change as a firm because your business context changes. It isn't that you wake up one morning and suddenly find yourself in trouble. Most business failures occur because leadership does not respond to long-term social and economic forces. Effective leaders have a clear vision of an industry's future and how a company can capitalize on change.

RS: What lessons have you learned in leading organizations through periods of radical transformation?

JN: People often misunderstand the purpose of large-scale change. Our change effort, Ford 2000, is perceived by some as a way to reduce costs and better leverage our resources. These are important goals. But what we really want to achieve is a new business philosophy and process—not a new organizational structure. The new organization is really a by-product of a much more fundamental shift to a global mind-set and approach. Many companies change their structures every few years without dealing with the fundamental assumptions and values that need to change. Consequently, they fail to achieve their long-term objectives.

We are seeking deep-level change in three areas. First, we want a global mind-set. That doesn't mean we ignore local markets; quite the contrary, it says that we must have effective strategies, rigorous practices, and talented people in every market. Second, we want everyone to see that we are a growth business. This is a very large industry with tremendous opportunities, and they don't all necessarily have to be in the core of our traditional business. Third, our actions reinforce that we must embrace change as a company. Stability is our enemy. In other words, some instability is needed to produce creative and innovative approaches to growing the business.

RS: One of your mantras is "focus." How do you integrate a diverse group of people and organizations and keep them aligned around your vital few imperatives?

JN: It is critical that everyone understands the fundamentals of the business. In larger organizations, many people view the business only from the narrow perspective of their functional assignments or geographical locations. They lose sight of the broader picture. As a result, they make shortsighted decisions or elevate too many unresolved issues to senior levels of management. This slows decision making and erodes accountability.

We want people to make the link between the business environment, the needs of our customers and shareholders, and their day-to-day work activities. To do this, you need to answer some fundamental questions:

What are the competitive forces that will change our industry?

What has the greatest impact on business results and what is relatively unimportant despite conventional wisdom?

Why is it necessary to look at the profitability of our various business segments?

What is cash flow and what do we mean by asset intensity?

These issues should concern every member of the organization. One role we play as leaders is to provide people with the context and information they need to answer such questions.

RS: Many organizations have performance targets that are well communicated. IBM in the early 1990s had very clear objectives and very poor results. How do you make your objectives more than inspirational rhetoric?

JN: I don't push targets on people. I push for agreement in regard to the competitive landscape and how we can be winners. Our priorities and milestones are deployed throughout the organization using our Business Enterprise Model. We closely link major process in our business to what really matters to people. For example, one core process is what we call "The Affordable Business Structure." It is a simple concept that starts with two fundamental questions: (1) What can the customer afford for a particular product? and (2) What are our shareholders' expectations for a return on their investment? Answering these questions gives us an affordable business model rather than a "cost plus" approach where some incorrectly assume that any cost can be passed on to customers.

People throughout the organization can take our management tools and evaluate what is needed within their areas of responsibility. We want a disciplined approach to making key decisions. For example, I was walking the factory line in one of our plants and an employee called me over and wanted to show me something. He knew the target cost of the engine within our Affordable Business Structure as well as its present cost. We went over how he and his team were addressing the gaps in our competitive cost structure. It is an example of what we are striving to accomplish in making our strategies come alive within the organization.

RS: Ford has developed a close working relationship with its employees and the UAW union. What are the keys to building this type of relationship?

JN: The bonds we see today were forged during the early 1980s when the survival of our company was at stake. In a crisis, we learned to work together. What sets the Ford-UAW relationship apart are the real business partnerships that you find from the top of the company to work teams in plants across the country. We share a great deal of information about the financial health of the firm and involve people in setting our long-term objectives. There is ongoing dialogue about the risks and opportunities we face, and we strive to create an environment that gives people autonomy to determine how best to meet our business objectives.

RS: You become frustrated when groups within your company compete against each other and miss opportunities to beat the outside competition. What have you found to be successful in building collaboration?

JN: One technique I use to enhance cross-group teamwork is to get leaders to work together on specific assignments. Instead of talking about teamwork, put people in situations that demand it. You take two or three people, or a small team, and give them a real-world problem that forces them to work together. They get to know each other and trust one another's judgment. Second, I am a strong believer in having people share common work areas. I learned early in my career that people working closely together have a lot of informal discussions—bumping into each other in the hallway or sharing a coffee. This creates a community around the business that is very powerful.

We use teams at every level of the organization. They are part of the reason we have improved our performance on key cost, speed, and quality targets. One interesting aspect of our recent improvements is that we have improved quality at the same time as we have reduced costs and become faster. Teams have helped generate energy and commitment to key business strategies. They also help ensure alignment and follow-through on objectives. But teams should not be used as a way to avoid tough decisions that, in some cases, require forceful leadership. You can go too far in striving for consensus on every issue. I have seen leaders take the path of least resistance to gain agreement among team members. The resulting decisions usually don't improve the competitiveness of the firm. There has to be leadership in the end, and it has to be clear that certain decisions will be the leader's.

RS: How do you identify and develop your emerging leaders?

JN: Our future leaders have to be technically superior in their chosen functions—whether it's a brilliant financial mind, a wonderful sense of marketing, or an eye for product engineering or design. Equally important, however, is the ability to understand the broader business context and the many forces that influence a business's success. Then you can achieve the appropriate balance between the competing needs of the enterprise.

We also encourage those striving to be leaders to take assignments outside their functional area or region. Such assignments result in a deep understanding of customers and the essence of the business from a profit-and-loss perspective. We want our people to seize every opportunity to interact with customers, suppliers, and employees in key functions and regions around the world. Leaders must be able to work across the company, across different groups, to solve key issues. Those who can do that are the most valued members of any team because they are versatile and open to change, quick and agile in their approach, and able to achieve results quickly.

RS: Ford was one of the first firms to establish global operations in the early decades of the 20th century. What has been the impact on how you view diversity in leadership?

JN: One of our competitive strengths is that we are an extremely diverse company. I recognize that we need to make more progress in leveraging our diversity. However, we understand the potential better than most firms. Diversity results in a more creative and vital culture. For example, my senior team comprises people from every region of the world. We need diverse points of view to understand and act on our global opportunities and challenges. There is not much point in having a team come together when everyone looks, acts, and talks the same. You get the maximum benefit when you have people with different views, backgrounds, personalities, and skills. There are companies, some our competitors, that are very homogeneous in their makeup. This can be a short-term strength because it is easier to get people who are alike to work together, make decisions, and act quickly on changes. However, a lack of diversity ultimately hinders a firm's long-term ability to anticipate and react to rapidly changing market conditions and customer wants.

RS: What have you found to be most challenging in developing future leaders?

JN: As a rule, we wait too long to test people and are too conservative in our approach. Many senior leaders fear a negative business impact when taking risks on unproven talent. They also fear offending those whose tenure suggests that they are next in line for a promotion or developmental opportunity. We must balance potential with experience in every team. Still, we should allow people early in their careers to take risks and face challenges that will develop them as leaders. Nothing produces as much learning and confidence as a challenging job assignment. There has to be a good way of handling the failures that will occur, and to make sure mistakes are not fatal to the careers of our emerging leaders.

Just as you need an intuitive feel for the business, our senior executives need to develop an intuitive feel for leadership potential. In the end you need to make judgments about people without having all the data you would like. That is one reason I strive to stay in touch with as many people as possible within the organization. I don't want information filtered through levels of management. I want to see our future leaders in person and watch them work through difficult challenges. We have plenty of leadership in this organization; what is required is our persistence in aggressively developing the talent that exists at every level of the organization.

RS: With the responsibility of leadership come praise and blame—some fairly earned, some not. What motivates you as a leader?

JN: Early in my career, I was willing to take assignments and risks that some avoided. I was less concerned with how people viewed me and more concerned with developing my own leadership skills and making our organization stronger. We now have an opportunity to become the preeminent automotive company in the world. That's exciting. But the next decade in the automotive industry is going to be as tough as any in our past. And, with strong global competitors such as Toyota and VW, we understand that the journey will not be easy.

Our role as leaders is to act on the most significant opportunities for growth. We know that the decisions we make will affect people all over the world: our employees, dealers, and suppliers; our customers and shareowners; the communities of which we are part. Many are depending upon us to demonstrate the leadership required for us to prosper into the next century. I wouldn't want it any other way.

Jacques Nasser was president and chief executive officer of Ford Motor Company until he was replaced by Henry Ford IV in October 2001. He had joined Ford of Australia in 1968 as a financial analyst. Nasser held numerous positions with Ford's Asian, South American, and European operations, including president of Ford of Australia, chairman of Ford of Europe, head of Ford's global product development, and head of Ford's global automotive operations.

Robert Shaw consults with senior executive teams on business strategy, organizational design, and large-scale change. His most recent book is *Trust in the Balance: Building Successful Organizations on Results, Integrity and Concern*.

10

Strategic Generosity

Leonard L. Berry

A study of outstanding service companies reveals ways to innovate, respond to customer needs, and energize employees. The leader's first job is to articulate a compelling and directional vision. Humane values guide decision making and action; they inspire and energize. High standards, innovation, teamwork, respect, joy, integrity, and social profit are part of values-driven leadership. A spirit of generosity extends to employees, partners, internal and external customers, and the community and builds emotional commitment and service excellence. Organizational success is measured by financial goals, customer satisfaction, employee growth and development, and innovation. People challenge the status quo and challenge the organization to improve. There is a long-term perspective, and shareholders who make a commitment to the organization are rewarded with value over time.

Serving the public is demanding, often frustrating, physically taxing work. Service excellence requires consistent execution, great systems, and, most of all, well-trained and committed people who can act on behalf of customers. How does a service organization achieve this perfection? How do leaders support the human energy, entrepreneurship, innovation, and boldness necessary to sustain excellence in today's world?

A study of 14 stellar service companies—and interviews with 250 of their employees, from CEOs to frontline workers—suggests some answers. This sample of world-class companies, drawn from hundreds of high-performing organizations, operates in many different settings. It includes a minor league baseball team, a small hotel group, a quick service restaurant chain, a regional airline, and a securities brokerage (see table). Yet the companies in the sample all create value for customers with labor-intensive service, have a record of sustained success, and share strikingly similar approaches to business.

Collectively they have now been in business for 435 years—an average of 31 years each—and have been profitable for 429 of those years. They have overcome the maladies that afflict so many organizations that mature and grow—additional layers of management, adoption of more formal (and less flexible) processes, and the loss of entrepreneurial zeal. Such afflictions make it even more difficult for organizations to sustain service excellence than to achieve it in the first place. Yet these 14 companies have actually become better over time, by continuing to innovate, respond to customer needs, and energize employees.

Values That Add Value

Nine drivers for sustained service excellence are evident in each of the companies I studied (see figure, p. 129). At the heart of their model of success is *values-driven leadership*—a set of enduring ideals, principles, and beliefs that guide decision making and action. These values are, above all, humane. Humane values inspire. They energize. They celebrate the potential of individuals to achieve, to excel, to grow, to love. Ultimately, service organizations—both for-profit and nonprofit—market *performances*.

Benchmark Companies for Study

Company	Headquarters	Principal Business	1997 Revenues ($ million)	Number of Employees
Bergstrom Hotels	Appleton, Wisconsin	Hotels	25	840
Charles Schwab	San Francisco	Securities brokerage and financial services	2,299	12,000
Chick-fil-A	Atlanta	Quick service restaurants	672	40,000 (300 at HQ)
The Container Store	Dallas	Specialty retailer	150	1,500
Custom Research	Minneapolis	Marketing research	26	120
Dana Commercial Credit	Toledo, Ohio	Leasing	2,000	750
Dial-A-Mattress	Long Island City, New York	Bedding retailer	70	250
Enterprise Rent-A-Car	St. Louis	Car rental	3,680	35,000
Midwest Express Airlines	Oak Creek, Wisconsin	Airline	345	2,300
Miller SQA	Holland, Michigan	Office furniture manufacturer	198	720
Special Expeditions	New York City	Expedition travel	52	167
St. Paul Saints	St. Paul, Minnesota	Professional baseball team	5	10
Ukrop's Super Markets	Richmond, Virginia	Food retailer	Not available	5,500
USAA	San Antonio, Texas	Insurance and financial services	7,454	18,500

A Snapshot of Sustained Service Excellence

They create value through personal interaction with their customers, usually without management supervision, in countless "moments of truth" day in and day out. Such performances are supported by seven ideals that collectively define "values-driven leadership" in these benchmark companies:

- *Excellence*—insisting on exceptionally high standards throughout the enterprise
- *Innovation*—changing the status quo into something better
- *Joy*—lifting the human spirit
- *Teamwork*—collaboratively pooling resources in a common purpose
- *Respect*—investing dignity and esteem, for customers and those who serve them, into the business process
- *Integrity*—competing on the basis of honesty and fair play
- *Social profit*—creating a net gain for society beyond the marketing of goods and services and the creation of jobs

Redefining Generosity

Another of the nine drivers of sustained success—and essential to values-driven leadership—is a spirit and practice that can only be described as *generous*. Generosity is usually thought of as something peripheral to the real concerns of a business. It is seen as a benevolent, philanthropic gesture, an incidental outcome of successful business. But in great service companies generosity is not just a *result* of business success *but a driver of the*

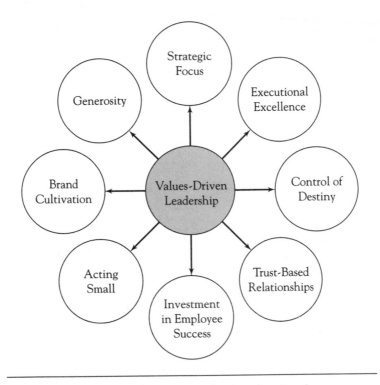

Drivers of Sustainable Success in Service Businesses
Source: Discovering the Soul of Service, p. 17.

success of the business. It is an expression of the leaders' humane values and a way to reinforce and enrich those values for employees and the community.

All the companies that sustained service excellence were uncommonly generous—with employees, partners, customers, the community. These companies understand that generous acts inspire people and that inspiration is essential to sustaining excellence. The founders of the Container Store, for instance, say that their number one value is, "Fill the other person's basket to the brim, and making money becomes an easy proposition."

They define "the other person" as anyone—the customer, colleague, vendor, community—they work with.

Custom Research, a $26 million marketing research company with 125 employees, won the National Malcolm Baldrige Award in 1996—at the time the smallest company to win. In April 1998, to thank their staff for a record year, owners Jeff Pope and Judy Corson took the entire staff on a five-day, all-expense-paid trip to London. "It was money well spent," says Pope. "I'll do it every time." Adds Corson, "If you share the pie, it gets bigger."

Midwest Express Airlines went public in 1995. Over the objections of its investment bankers, CEO Tim Hoeksema insisted that $1 million in stock be set aside for employees. Every employee, including the part-timers, was given a stake in the company—based on years of seniority, not rank. He went to bat for the people who had made the company successful, and that story is now part of the lore—and the lure—of the company.

Ukrop's Super Markets, a family-owned chain based in Richmond, Virginia, donates 10 percent of its pretax profits to the community. Another 20 percent is earmarked for employees' quarterly bonuses, and 10 percent more for long-term profit sharing. The company donated $500,000 to establish a culinary education center in a local community college. Many of the people who go through that course wind up working for Ukrop's, which sells freshly prepared food and baked goods as well as groceries.

Chick-fil-A founder Truett Cathy gives $1,000 college scholarships to selected employees who are enrolled in school, perform well on the job, and complete a year of work. At a time when so many companies are posting "help wanted" signs, Chick-fil-A is attracting capable, college-bound people. Between 1973 and 1997 the company gave away nearly $13 million in scholarships.

True generosity is a mark of great companies from day one and does not depend on the momentary fortunes of the giver. (When Cathy opened his first restaurant, with little money and an uncertain future, he treated every employee, including back office staff, to lunch every day.) Generosity is woven into the fabric of these companies' business and strategy, their future. It is a genuine expression of their values, but it turns out to also make good business sense. To serve the customer, you have to first serve the service provider. Selfish companies cannot serve either.

Providing a steady paycheck is enough for mediocrity. But excellence demands more. Excellence requires inspiration. When your product is performance, you must rely on the discretionary efforts of your performers, and on their commitment to customers, to each other, and to the company. That is why organizations that sustain excellence first become inspirational places to work.

Building Emotional Commitment

The way to lead people to sustained service excellence is to create an atmosphere in which they become emotionally involved in their work. Strategic generosity is one way you do that. You also do it through the kind of workplace you create—the quality of your practices and opportunities—and through the dream you offer. A dream—the cause around which people organize their efforts—can be created around seemingly mundane products or services. And it can elevate that service into something more. For example, Dial-A-Mattress is, on the surface, not a particularly inspiring business. Yet its people value their role in providing an essential service with integrity and innovation.

Dial-A-Mattress sells bedding over the phone, 24 hours a day. It is creating a national distribution network that can deliver orders within two hours. Its people take the old mattress away, deliver the new mattress (or two, for customers who want to try more than one), and offer a 30-day satisfaction guarantee. Founder Napoleon Barragan's dream is to make it easy for customers to buy a product that typically is difficult to buy. One of his everyday jobs as a leader is to reinforce and remind everybody—longtime and new employees—of the company's reason for being (see "Tasks of Values-Driven Leaders").

Joyful, energetic organizations often depend on the vision and personality of a leader. Yet they sustain their vision and values beyond that person. Company founder Charles Schwab, for instance, is revered in his company. But he created systems and built values that will sustain themselves long after he is gone. Contrary to industry practice, Schwab does not pay sales commissions. Sales representatives earn bonuses based on their customer service performance and the assets they attract to the firm. Temptations to churn accounts or sell particular investment vehicles do not exist.

Tasks of
Values-Driven Leaders

All organizations that sustain service excellence have a dream. It is clear, compelling, and directional. The leader's first job is to paint a picture of that destination. Written expressions of the dream are rarely potent in and of themselves. They are potent and credible only if everything that is unwritten—practices, assumptions, and the day-to-day behavior of leaders—reinforces what's written. But if the behavior is inconsistent, then the words are hollow.

Another role of a values-driven leader is to define organizational success and remind everybody in the company of the true measures of the organization's progress. Is it simply profit, market share, or share price? Or are there other measures as well? The companies I studied complement financial goals with additional measures of success, such as customer satisfaction, employee growth and development, and innovation.

To create sustainable excellence in a company, leaders cultivate other leaders throughout the organization. We have it wrong when we use the phrase "middle management"; what we need is *middle leadership*. Most of the people in an organization work for the people in the middle, not for the people at the top. Cultivating middle leadership is a key role of values-driven leaders.

Leaders assert values in good times and bad. When a company is going through a difficult period, core values provide guidance. They help us make the tough calls. Yet, ironically, it may be easier to embrace core values in times of crisis than to continually assert those values—to challenge the status quo and challenge the organization to improve—during periods of relative normalcy. That is why so many values-driven leaders fear complacency and why they find ways to foment ongoing change. At Charles Schwab, for instance, there *is* no status quo. People are always working on the next thing—inventing a new technology, investing in R&D, trying to improve on what they do, and maintaining an entrepreneurial edge.

One of the ways effective leaders implement and sustain core values is to recruit people who share those values. Though the workforces of top-performing companies are demographically, educationally, ethnically, and socially diverse, they have a strong commonality of values. When a company makes a good hire, it brings into the company someone who strives for excellence, is looking for a joyful workplace, is respectful toward others, is a team player, and has integrity.

Knowing Who's in Charge

Great organizations find ways to control their own destiny, even if they are publicly traded corporations. They maintain a strong organizational identity. Asked "Who is the boss?"—they answer with the face of the customer. But in a service business, there are two key customer groups: the service providers and the served. Generously serving both customers is the best way to build shared values and to stay independent.

Great public companies serve another key constituency—long-term shareowners (not day traders or short-term speculators, whom the company owes nothing beyond an honest financial statement). People making a commitment to the company are the true owners, and you serve them best by creating economic value over time. Too many public companies, without admitting it, are managed for the short-term results necessary to satisfy the investment community. It takes bold, courageous, and generous leaders to be mindful of short-term needs but to focus on long-term sustainability.

To be sure, public companies that miss their quarterly or annual earnings estimates pay a real, and often severe, price. However, to build a company for the future, to pursue true excellence, and to inspire people to achieve things they'd never thought possible requires decisions today that will strengthen the company tomorrow. Effective leaders educate investors about their strategy, make the case for long-term investment, and then deliver results.

Contrast the experience of ValuJet, which made over $20 million in 1994, its first full year of operation, with Southwest Airlines, which earned that much only after eight years of operation, starting in 1971. Today ValuJet is a small player forced to adopt a new name, and Southwest is one of our great airlines. You build excellence slowly and consistently. That doesn't give you license to be foolish or wasteful, but it does suggest that you manage your intangible assets as wisely as your financial ones. Jeff Pope and Judy Corson don't think they wasted money taking 125 people to London. They see a return in an inspired workforce, consistent profitability, a Baldrige award, and a sterling client list that includes companies such as Coca-Cola and Procter & Gamble.

Leaders of great organizations know the value that their people generate in their lasting relationships with customers. They master the balancing act between the short term and the long term and among their multiple stakeholder groups. They decide early on what is important and who is the boss, and they craft strategies accordingly. They honor the values that must endure even as the organization evolves. That is the only way to win the hearts of those they lead. And over the long life of a great organization, winning hearts is the only way to serve others well.

Leonard L. Berry holds the M. B. Zale Chair in Retailing and Marketing Leadership and is distinguished professor of marketing at the Lowry Mays College and Graduate School of Business, Texas A&M University. A prolific writer on services, he is author of numerous articles and books on service excellence, including *On Great Service* and, most recently, *Discovering the Soul of Service*.

11

Creating Your Next Business Model

Adrian Slywotzky

Value migration—the shift of market value from one company to another—follows the creation of a better business model. A critical skill is identifying profit zones—new areas in which to serve customers profitably. In this arena, strategy is as important as technology. Successful companies examine their strategic assumptions; changes in demographic, social, and political forces; changes in customer needs and priorities; and opportunities for profit. And they change their business models every four or five years, before it becomes economically necessary to do so. They identify the customers who will have the greatest impact on future success in the industry and build their next-generation business model around those customers. Then they reinvent themselves and realign to support their new business models and make themselves the first choice of these customers.

The rules that define business success have changed. Today all organizations face competitive challenges that threaten seemingly indomitable leaders. Yet companies that understand the changing rules of the game can be more successful than ever.

Just 15 years ago, the classic laws of business strategy worked well: gain relative market share and the profit will follow. But since the 1980s those rules have broken down, as IBM, Digital Equipment, Eastman Kodak, United Airlines, U.S. Steel, General Motors, Ford, and many others can attest. These players won market share and grossed top revenues in their industries but failed to earn profits. Instead, aggressive competitors developed strategies that created new value for customers, shareholders, and partners.

The shift of market value from one company to another follows one factor above all others—the creation of a better business model. Leaders who understand this process of "value migration" can better answer such essential questions as

Where will we be allowed to earn a profit in our industry?

How do changes in customers redefine that opportunity?

What's the next-generation business model for our industry?

How must we innovate to capture and protect our financial future? What new way of doing business will we have to invent?

Of course, profit is not the sole measure of success, but it is essential to any business. Profit and market value—the value of all outstanding shares of a company's stock—also provide objective measures of performance, not only for investors but for employees, suppliers, regulators, and the communities in which businesses operate. Market value reflects investor confidence in the future of a company, and a dramatic increase in market value can signal important changes in a marketplace, an industry, or an entire economy. Any company that sustains growth in its market value far beyond the performance of the broad market probably has something to teach others.

The No-Profit Zone

The best example of value migration is the computing industry, where the dominant business model was well established by 1980: sell systems around a central processor, using proprietary technology and a direct sales force. But from 1982 to 1992, this model lost over $90 billion in shareholder value. Did that value simply disappear or accrue to the customer? Not at all. During the same period, a handful of companies using new business designs increased their shareholder value by more than $300 billion.

One explanation for this astounding shift of wealth is improved technology. But that hardly accounts for the scope of the phenomenon. Is Intel's success due to inherently better computer chips than, say, Advanced Micro Devices'—or to a carefully crafted business design that creates and maintains a two-year product lead over competitors? Is Microsoft's Windows operating system really better than the Macintosh operating system? Or is its success a function of a unique business design that combines a de facto standard, a suite of applications, and the industry's most aggressive investment in support for application developers? Perhaps better than any organization, Microsoft understands the need to always consider its next-generation business model. It is adept at identifying profit zones—new areas in which it can serve customers profitably. Microsoft's dominance is based on brilliant strategy, not brilliant technology.

Failure to fundamentally rethink one's business model has turned entire markets into no-profit zones. In the airline industry, for example, net profit generation has been zero for the past 20 years. Most companies have had a few good years, and a few companies—very few—have had many good years. But overall, the industry has not earned a dime. Over the past 15 years, the same has been true of the automotive industry, consumer electronics, home insurance, and many others. And the trend is growing. To assure the long-term health of their organization, leaders must determine whether the market they serve is becoming structurally unprofitable and then must either exit that market or change their business model accordingly.

Consider Coca-Cola, arguably the most powerful brand in the world. Coke sells in three channels in the United States—grocery stores, fountains, and vending machines. Its greatest volume comes from groceries. But that is the least profitable segment of its business. A Coke bought in a vending machine costs 5 to 7 cents per ounce; from a restaurant fountain the same 12 ounces of soda costs 6 to 10 cents per ounce. But from a grocery store, it costs no more than 2 cents per ounce. The most powerful brand and one of the most profitable products in the world has as its largest single business a huge no-profit zone. Can Coke walk away from the grocery business? Hardly. But the company has reinvented its business model to take full advantage of the profitability in other parts of its domestic market—and has focused even more effort on the far more attractive overseas market. In 1997, Coke made about $4 billion in profit, 85 percent of it internationally.

Creating New Value

In the years ahead, companies that fail to identify such opportunities will find to their dismay that sustained competitive advantage is becoming impossible. Research shows that only about a dozen large corporations (including Charles Schwab, Coca-Cola, Walt Disney, General Electric, Intel, and Microsoft) have achieved high long-term growth of market value by redesigning their business model. Collectively, this handful of companies created over $700 billion of value growth in 15 years—more than 10 percent of the stock market value created since 1982. They outperformed traditional market-share leaders across such diverse industries as computing, automobiles, steel, air travel, and entertainment. While market-share leaders grew value at about 7 percent a year and the Standard & Poor's 500 index at about 11 percent, the reinventors grew at 23 percent a year for 15 years. Even excluding extraordinary performers like Microsoft and Intel, stock price growth among these companies remains close to 20 percent a year.

These companies share at least two traits. They tend to change their business model every four to five years, a year or two before it becomes economically necessary to do so. And they routinely reverse traditional strategic thinking. They don't start by asking how to increase their market share; they ask instead, "How does profit really happen in our industry, and how do we build a business model that takes advantage of that profitability?"

In 1981, when the late Roberto Goizueta became CEO of Coca-Cola, it was essentially a syrup maker and advertiser, selling through franchise bottlers who often had their own business models. Fountain and vending machines were largely controlled by local bottlers. When Coca-Cola began to rethink its business, its senior managers often spoke of "the curse of the revenue line." They meant to focus people's attention not on revenue, not on market share, but on first understanding how profit happened and how their business model had to change to assure profitability.

The company started purchasing bottlers, consolidating them, modernizing them, and by the mid-1980s had become not simply a syrup maker and advertiser but rather a value-chain manager. The company recognized that the intense competition and low returns in the supermarket provided limited profitability but that the supermarket position was a cornerstone on which to build other businesses. Today, in an industry that grows only about 3 percent in the United States and 7 percent to 8 percent internationally, Coca-Cola has grown its market value at a compounded annual rate of 26 percent over 15 years.

Focusing on Best Customers

Coca-Cola is exceptional, not only in the intensity and clarity of its thinking about profitability but also in its focus on thinking strategically about customers. The company has many customers—from bottlers to grocers to fountain owners to vending location owners to consumers—and there are many types of customers within each of those categories. But like all reinventors, the company challenges assumptions by focusing not on all customers but on *the most important customer*. Managers identify the customers that will have the greatest impact on future success in the industry, and they build their next-generation business model around those customers (see table).

Coca-Cola solved its profitability problem using a multicomponent business model; it operates many lines of business but concentrates on those that represent a disproportionate share of its profits. Another industry reinventor, Walt Disney Company, adopted a different model to solve a different business problem. Disney always created value in its industry, but other companies used its products to capture even greater value. In the mid-1980s,

Strategic innovators such as the following companies build new business models by answering the question, "Who is our most important customer?"

	Not Just	But Also
Charles Schwab	Investors	Financial planners, regional banks, regional brokers
Coca-Cola	Consumers	Key bottlers
General Electric	Purchasing agents	Solution seekers
Intel	Original equipment makers	End users
Microsoft	Consumers	Application developers, original equipment manufacturers
Walt Disney	Children	Families

Innovation in Customer Selection
Source: Mercer Management Consulting

when Michael Eisner became CEO, Disney developed film content, characters, and intellectual property, which it licensed to manufacturers and retailers. Disney had no stake in those retail channels, and its earnings from licensing were modest by industry standards—$16 million profit on $100 million in revenue. Recognizing that other parts of the distribution system were benefiting from the value that Disney was creating, Eisner led a difficult transition, concentrating the company's core competencies while learning critical new ones. The company mastered the art and science of retailing. By opening its own stores, Disney not only improved profitability but also gained a stronger negotiating position with manufacturers and other retailers and, as important, delivered a better experience to consumers by transporting the Disney mystique into the retail environment.

The impact was dramatic. Within 10 years Disney's licensing and retailing revenues grew to $1.8 billion, and profits reached $500 million. One of many examples of Disney's integrated system is *The Lion King,* one of the most successful movies of all time. It generated an impressive $400 million at the box office, but that was just the beginning—total revenue from all ancillary activities was close to $2 billion.

Disney developed a "profit multiplier model," reapplying its key assets in the form of many spin-off products and services. As with Coca-Cola, the valuation of the company has soared relative to industry peers. However, a given business model can have economic vitality for only a few years before competitors start to imitate it and drain value. Thus, while Coca-Cola, Disney, and the other industry reinventors each makes a profit in a different way, they all understand that they must continually innovate to stay ahead of changing conditions in their industry.

To avoid falling into a no-profit zone in your industry, ask yourself and your colleagues a series of questions:

How are financial results achieved in your business?

Who are your customers, and how are their priorities changing?

What is the model by which your organization competes?

Is there only one model, or are there other models?

Is your organization aligned to support its business model?

And will your business model today endure, or will you need to invent a different way of achieving results tomorrow?

Nonprofit and government leaders can ask similar questions about how to produce value for customers, results for funders, and meaningful change in communities. They must constantly question what needs they can best address and how those needs are changing in the face of social, economic, demographic, and political forces. Having the right business model is as important for public and social sector organizations as for companies.

The city of Indianapolis has invented a new model for the delivery of street repair, sanitation, and other public services, asking city agencies to compete with the private sector and sharing the significant productivity savings with both citizens and employees. Regis University, in Denver, developed a new learning model by offering its adult education expertise to local businesses. The school's on-site program directors manage the learning needs of the client's workforce, erasing the distinctions between school and company. Regis has thus secured its once-tenuous financial future and now counts not just teaching but *partnering* as one of its core competencies.

Reinventors concentrate on the unique way they create value for customers and investors. They do so by taking a fundamentally different approach to three dimensions of business strategy. First, they do not start by trying to gain market share, but by building the right business model. They know that huge market share with the wrong business model is more of a liability than an asset. Second, they give priority not to their product or technology but to their customers, and they think about how to become their best customers' preferred choice. Finally, they do not start developing strategy based on what they are good at today. They start by asking what they need to learn to excel in the future. They know they will have to keep changing their business design to stay ahead of the changes in customers, competitors, and the economics of their industry.

General Electric, for instance, probably knows better than anyone how manufacturers make money. Yet it has fundamentally changed its business design since 1982. In the early years of Jack Welch's tenure, the business model was based on the principle "Be No. 1 or No. 2 in a market or get out." At that time, being the market share leader was clearly the path to highest profitability. By the mid-1980s, however, that changed. The customers that GE sells to—Wal-Mart, Ford, GM, Boeing—are unimpressed with the fact that a supplier has a leading market position; they'd rather get the best price. This customer expectation led GE to declare a new goal: to be No. 1 not just in market share but also in productivity, through Work-Out and other organizational innovations. Welch saw that top market share without the best productivity would no longer assure profitability.

But by the early 1990s even that was no longer enough. A trip around the world convinced Welch of some profound market shifts: there was too much manufacturing capacity in the world, market power had swung from suppliers to customers, and too many companies were competing in the same ways. GE started looking beyond its market position and productivity strategies—both of which were built on manufacturing—to yet another model. The company shifted its focus to the development of services, solutions, and other ancillary activities, inventing offerings that helped customers improve the economic equation of their total system. Today, GE earns its greatest profits from financial services, leasing, and support services rather than from the industrial and consumer products of the past.

The Courage to Change

Ultimately, customer focus reduces business risk. By habitually changing their business design, reinventors avoid the crises that befall market leaders caught unaware by structural changes in their industry.

In short, all successful organizations have to protect their future viability by constantly reassessing how they provide value to customers and then designing their business to best deliver that value. It is a process of creating unique forms of knowledge—about the customer and the nature of the marketplace—and translating that knowledge into value.

The rules have fundamentally changed and are continuing to change. Combining a strategic understanding of one's business model with an organization-wide understanding of the customer is much harder to do than simply increasing market share. But that thinking and the actions that follow from it bring incredible rewards. Fifteen years ago it was extraordinarily difficult to overturn established market leaders. There was great creativity in technology but little creativity in business design innovation. What will be different about business in the next five years is strategic imagination. Business reinventors create a unique business model in their field, and when that uniqueness is threatened by imitation, they move on. They design a new model that makes them the first choice of their most important customers.

These companies offer lessons in strategic innovation, to be sure. But they are also reminders of the leadership, courage, and vision of men and women who fought the inertia and skepticism within their own organization and the uncertainty of outside forces. We can take advantage of the learning they've created to develop techniques and processes for innovation. But most important, we can adopt their style of thought as we reinvent our own organizations—as we must to assure a viable future.

Adrian Slywotzky is a vice president at Mercer Management Consulting. He works with chief executives of major corporations on business strategy and design, focusing on business development and value growth in changing markets. He is a frequent speaker, author of *Value Migration*, and coauthor of the best-selling *The Profit Zone*, and *How Digital Is Your Business?*

12

Principles for Partnership

James E. Austin

Businesses are being asked to take more responsibility for the well-being of the communities in which they operate. Because healthy communities are a competitive advantage in recruitment and retention, in organizational image, and in the vibrancy of the marketplace, public-private partnerships are a form of long-range planning. To make such partnerships work, leaders must ensure participation, build relationships, create value, and achieve accountability.

The problems facing our cities seem to defy solution. But the only certainty is that these increasingly complex challenges exceed the capabilities of any single sector—public, private, or nonprofit—to solve them alone.

At the same time that the public is asking government and nonprofit organizations to be more effective, produce demonstrable results, and make more of the public and philanthropic capital invested in them, it is also asking businesses to take more responsibility for the well-being of the communities in which they operate. Given these heightened demands, more and more leaders are finding an innovative answer both to community problems and to the furtherance of their own long-term interests.

"Public-private partnership is the answer," says Robert Gillespie, head of KeyCorp and chairman of Cleveland Tomorrow, a coalition that works to revitalize that city. "I don't know of any of my peers who think any of this could have been done by the business community alone. If you don't have that kind of partnership, you shouldn't bother trying, because it simply can't be done." Gillespie isn't alone in this view. Increasingly, leaders are seeing that functions that might have been viewed as clearly the government's domain, such as public education or public safety, also require attention from the business and nonprofit sectors. Cross-sector partnering between business, government, and nonprofits will be the collaboration paradigm of the 21st century.

Why Businesses Get Involved

There are many motivations that lead business leaders to support a public partnership. Larry Perlman, CEO of Ceridian Corporation, speaks for many in making the case for social engagement: "A corporation in this world today carries with it a responsibility broader than just running the business every day. Business will not endure in a society that's not functional, so in a sense it's the most effective form of long-range strategic planning." Leaders cite four specific reasons for getting involved.

Healthy communities are a competitive advantage. In the intensified global competition for talent, the quality of the community in which an organization operates can create a competitive edge. Morton Mandel, former CEO of Premier Industrial Corporation, explains that his business community's activism was "fueled by our growing concern about the image Cleveland had nationally and internationally, and the impact of that image on how people might feel about joining our companies or relocating to Cleveland." Likewise, Marilyn Carlson Nelson, CEO of the $20 billion ✓ Carlson Companies, says, "The quality of life in the Twin Cities and in Minnesota is the differentiator for us. It is what attracts the best and the brightest. In this competitive environment we have all needed to create an extra edge for our community and ourselves." The message is clear: sick cities seldom produce a vibrant business sector.

Community service makes better leaders. Senior executives are finding they gain personal satisfaction from community engagement and enhance their leadership skills. General Mills CEO Steve Sanger points to three benefits: "One, you find that you can really contribute; two, you meet other people in the community that you enjoy interacting with, learning about, and getting to know; three, the time spent on problems away from direct business problems is helpful in giving you a broader perspective that helps you become a better leader within your organization. I tell people here all the time, 'We support your volunteering not just because we know you'll help the community but because we believe that volunteering helps you be a better leader.'"

Service is part of the local business culture. Some cities appear to have a long history of civic activism by business leaders, so community service is embedded in the business culture. In Minneapolis, James Campbell, president of Norwest Bank Minnesota, says, "There's something magical here, a feeling of responsibility, of giving back to the community and making everyone's life better. It is an ingrained expectation. One example is a global corporation that feels the incredible involvement of business leaders here. There is an inescapable expectation that every CEO must be involved in making this a better city." The effects of this long tradition can be powerful. Leaders build a base of shared values, learning, and experience that makes the business community itself more vibrant. Strong community service norms can be a powerful force shaping leaders' behavior.

Crises can trigger collaboration. In several cities crises catalyzed the business community into collective action. Boston and New York's fiscal crises and Cleveland's actual bankruptcy mobilized business leaders to become community activists. The anti-business positions of Boston's and Cleveland's mayors at that same time also sparked a political response, as the business leadership in those cities successfully supported opposition candidates more inclined to bring business and community interests together. Detroit Renaissance, that city's business leadership coalition, was formed in the aftermath of the inner-city riots in the late 1960s and began a collaborative effort with city government to rebuild and revitalize the urban center.

Making Collaboration Work

With the growth of public-private partnerships, we are learning what it takes to make them work. Indeed, we know that for cross-sector partnerships to work, leaders must ensure participation, build relationships, create value, and achieve accountability.

Ensuring participation. It was common in decades past for business leaders, often operating through business leadership coalitions, to exercise power secretively with their government counterparts. But that decision-making model, which had CEOs striking deals with mayors and governors behind the guarded doors of private clubs, has been disintegrating. As Thomas O'Brien, former chairman of Pittsburgh's Allegheny Conference on Community Development (ACCD), says, "It's not like the old days when banker Mellon and Mayor Lawrence would get together and just do it. You need to draw a much larger consensus to get things done. The real challenge is to broaden the participation to those sectors that are creating and driving a lot of the growth, and at the same time not to dilute the power or the effectiveness of the Conference."

Atlanta's business leadership coalition, Central Atlanta Progress (CAP), focused on expanding its sphere of influence by "building a bigger tent," as CAP's chairman, Duane Ackerman, chairman and CEO of BellSouth, puts it. The consolidation of businesses has also meant that some members are top executives of their companies in the area, but not the CEO. Charlie Battle, the current CAP president, says, "We have a much broader membership now. We are not just downtown organizations and we have everybody from huge corporations to nonprofits that are members. You have to put together those kinds of partnerships to make things happen."

The *process* of partnering can be as important as the substance. For example, in 1987 Detroit Renaissance proposed a strategic plan to tackle the city's social and economic problems comprehensively. Mayor Young took umbrage at the business leaders' unilateral presentation of the plan, as it made his administration appear unresponsive. Consequently he never supported the effort. (For an illustration of the importance of community participation, see "The Atlanta Project.")

Genuine participation in collective decision making fosters respect, and respect fosters trust. But Richard Stafford, ACCD's executive director, points to a trade-off: "The more inclusion you get, the more power to influence you have; but the less ability you have to come to a conclusion." Reaching consensus in a public-private partnership will often test the patience of business leaders used to quick decision-making processes. Entering into such partnerships is analogous to doing business in a foreign

The Atlanta Project

The Atlanta Project (TAP), started in 1991 with the support of Jimmy Carter and the Carter Center, has shown the importance of broad participation in any business leadership initiative. This effort aimed to create partnerships between leading corporations, universities, and specific neighborhoods in metropolitan Atlanta. President Carter's active promotion of TAP generated enthusiastic corporate support, much publicity, and high expectations. By 1996, many were disappointed by the slow progress, and only 10 of the 30 initial corporate sponsors continued with their community initiatives. Doug Greenwell, executive director of TAP from 1996 to 1999, explained that the well-intended projects of the corporate sponsors exceeded the absorptive capacity of the neighborhoods: "For there to be any significant social change in the neighborhood, the people who live there have to decide what that is going to be, and they have to be the ones who participate in making those changes."

Consequently, Phase II of TAP shifted its strategy dramatically toward "building community capacity." In effect, money, corporate skills, good intentions, and positive "can-do attitude" will not work if extended unilaterally without the active engagement of the community to ensure buy-in and implementation. The corporations that did continue on in TAP II—UPS, Ford, Delta Airlines, IBM, Sprint, Georgia Power, Turner Broadcasting, the Prudential Foundation, Atlanta Power and Light Co., and SunTrust Bank—developed deeper and more fruitful partnerships focused on problems identified as high priority by the neighborhoods.

As Greenwell put it, "TAP made everybody smarter." A local business leader provided perspective: "Nothing works without a wonderful joined-at-the-hip public-private partnership. All the money available to man is useless if you don't have the elected official support to make it work. You have got to be able to deal with these issues together."

country. The culture, the language, and the form of interaction are different, and the most successful international businesspeople are those who study, understand, and respect the different cultural norms and expectations. Furthermore, they learn at least the basics of the other's language and culture to communicate effectively. Their resultant broadening of leadership, communication, negotiating skills, and general knowledge makes them better managers back in the business.

Building relationships. The new partnerships of business and government and nonprofits do not just happen. They are built. As business statesman David Rockefeller put it, "One has to make an effort to get to know the leaders in government, and make them feel that you're not there as supplicants, but that you're there as citizens who are trying to work with them in jointly doing something to improve the city and the state." But Rockefeller also pointed out that "nonprofit and government leaders need to have a positive attitude towards business, be cooperative and not denigrating, and recognize the role of business is very important."

Relationships between business and government are often particularly fragile and can easily turn sour. A bridge-building mind-set and an array of political skills are critical for the executive directors of the business leadership coalitions. For example, the recently recruited executive directors of Detroit Renaissance and the Minnesota Business Partnership were formerly leaders in their states' legislatures and seen as highly skilled in relationship building. Similarly, the executive director of Central Atlanta Progress from the early 1970s to the late 1980s was described by a colleague as "steeped in the political wherewithal to get things done."

At the heart of strong relationships are respect and trust. A community leader and CAP member explains the difficulty:

"The biggest challenge is establishing an effective working relationship among all of the parties, principally business and government and the community activists. The community activists
basically don't trust the business people, and the businesspeople, in a sense, don't trust them. They don't trust our motives,
and we're not sure we trust their methods." ACCD's O'Brien,
based on his frequent interactions with the mayor of Pittsburgh,
counsels, "Even if you had a disagreement with the political
philosophy, you would still have said, 'We all live here and we
all want to make this a better place,' and throw those things
aside and work at it. The reason that we've been successful is
that we've got our hand into all the discussions with a basis of
trust—trust between the private and public sector."

Trust must be earned by actions. When populist-oriented Ray
Flynn was elected mayor of Boston in the mid-1980s, many of
Boston's corporate leaders were fearful of the anti-business stance
of some of Flynn's supporters. However, when the business leaders created a $5 million scholarship fund for Boston public school
students, Flynn declared with enthusiasm that the business community's effort "builds bridges of opportunity between downtown
and neighborhoods." The business community and Mayor Flynn
went on to have a productive and positive relationship during his
multiple terms in office. In Cleveland, in 1989, African American Michael White won a surprise victory for mayor without the
business community's support. Nonetheless, one of his early actions was to back a tax levy for the downtown sports complex
backed by the city's top business leaders. This politically risky
stance demonstrated his seriousness about cross-sector collaboration and earned him respect and support from the business leaders.

Creating value. The power of collaboration comes from
combining partners' core competencies in mutually reinforcing

ways. Business needs to contribute what it does best. Michael Bonsignore, CEO of Honeywell, says, "Getting the business community to step in alongside government and nonprofits—not to take responsibility away from them, but to bring management methods, communication, prioritization, structure, and discipline to allow them to function more effectively—ends up a huge win-win." Businesses have considerable competency in problem analysis and planning. The business leadership coalitions in Pittsburgh and Cleveland added value by providing higher-quality analysis of priority problems, often in partnership with local research centers. Both of these business leadership groups were also active in planning regional development strategies formulated with broad community participation.

Public-private collaboration in Minneapolis created the highest possible value—it saved lives. In the summer of 1996 the city was shocked by a record 40 murders. The *New York Times* labeled the city "Murderopolis" because its per capita homicide rate exceeded New York's. The governor sent the state's National Guard reserves into Minneapolis and asked Honeywell to help fund a consultant to work on this problem.

Instead of just paying for a consultant, Honeywell's CEO used his influence to mobilize a coalition of other business leaders, judges, law enforcement officials, community leaders, and nonprofit groups. The objective was simple: have a safer summer in 1997 than 1996. The group focused on immediate problems of guns, gangs, and drugs with a community prevention approach and also began tackling the structural problems of jobs, housing, and neighborhood revitalization. The coalition brought together groups that did not know one another, such as different law enforcement units and community organizations. The corporations helped coordinate efforts by providing management practices for interdepartmental communication, prioritization, and performance measurement to a diverse and dispersed set of public-sector institutions.

The coalition's effort (Hope, Education, Law & Safety, or HEALS) reduced the number of murders the next summer to seven and attracted the U.S. Attorney General and Secretary of Labor to the Twin Cities to see how complex problems can be tackled through cross-sector collaboration. Honeywell Foundation president Patricia Hoven explains, "It's not about money or Honeywell getting credit. It is about leveraging the unbelievable perceived leadership ability to bring multiple groups together and to be a bridge between the public and private sectors. . . . We are seen as an objective party, as are other business leaders in the coalition. Moreover, the second objective of creating jobs and revitalizing neighborhoods will never happen without private sector CEOs' being involved."

Achieving accountability. Effective partners expect a lot of each other. If results are not forthcoming, value is not being created. It is difficult to retain CEOs' time, attention, and resources if clear value is not returned on the investment. The recent demise of Boston's traditional business leadership coalition, tellingly known as "the Vault," is a case in point. The Vault's perceived elitist and secretive style meant that it was not answerable to a larger constituency. Other business leadership groups emerged with broader membership and visibility, greater influence, and more relevant agendas. In other cities, limited staff capacity in City Hall has impeded the mayor's ability to follow through on commitments made to the business community. One-sided contributions put partnerships at risk.

Of all the business leadership coalitions, Pittsburgh's ACCD has perhaps moved most aggressively in creating an accountability mechanism. In 1993 ACCD commissioned a white paper on economic revitalization by Robert Mehrabian, president of Carnegie Mellon University. This paper led to the 1994 formation of the Working Together Consortium (WTC), a committee with a representative cross-section of stakeholders from business, education, labor, public and community agencies, and philanthropies. ACCD works closely with WTC and some leaders sit on both boards. In addition to reporting on the community's progress on carrying out its economic development agenda, WTC also fosters the creation of other partnerships to implement the agenda.

Keeping the torch lit. Many communities and organizations are recognizing the need to engage the next generation of collaborators. This challenge has been complicated by the globalization of business, which not only has CEOs on the road more but also multiplies the number of communities companies are interacting with. The headquarters community does not have the same preferential call on corporate resources that it had in the past. Mergers and consolidations lead to larger and different companies, which often disrupts long-standing relationships between business leaders and their counterparts in the other sectors. There is increasing scarcity of CEO time. Thus, just as there are growing pressures and expectations for higher business engagement with the community, there are also conflicting constraints on such involvement. Carlson Companies CEO Marilyn Carlson Nelson says, "There are trends in business that are undermining our sense of place and threaten to undo the good so many have done. Our corporations, however global, must not be stateless—homeless. If that happens, our corporate cultures will be soulless and we will fail."

To address this challenge, some cities have created civic leadership development organizations (for example, Leadership Cleveland, Leadership Atlanta, and New York's David Rockefeller

Fellows Program) that engage upcoming leaders from the business, government, and social sectors in shared learning and interaction. The purposes are to increase their understanding of significant problems facing the communities, to create a network of relationships across the sectors, and to deepen their commitment to community stewardship. Margot Copeland, executive director of Leadership Cleveland, says, "The story of Cleveland's turnaround is how we cultivate the ground for leaders from different points of view to sit down and talk together, listen to each other, share information, and then agree on a common purpose." Some corporations lend executives to the business leadership coalitions or to government or nonprofit organizations to provide expertise—and also to enrich their professional development.

The growing recognition among corporations of the value of community service programs and cross-sector partnering suggests there is in our corporations a fertile environment for developing civic leadership. Interest among MBA students in community engagement and social enterprise has never been higher. Business leaders have an opportunity to signal both to emerging leaders in their companies and to incoming managers and staff that community engagement is integral to the ethic of true leadership. We may be witnessing the emergence of a new social contract between business and the rest of society through public-private partnerships. At a time when we know that no one sector holds the answers—that our future depends on working together—we really have no choice.

James E. Austin is John G. McLean Professor of Business Administration at Harvard University Graduate School of Business Administration. He is chair of the school's Initiative on

Social Enterprise and has served as an adviser to corporations, international agencies, and nonprofits, and as a special adviser to the White House. He has authored or edited 16 books, including *The Collaboration Challenge*.

The author thanks Harvard Business School research associates Arthur McCaffrey, Prakash Puram, Linda Carrigan, and Stephanie Woerner for their assistance.

13

Leadership in a Virtual World

Deborah L. Duarte and Nancy Tennant Snyder

Virtual teams offer many advantages. They can support projects that one organizational partner could not otherwise fund and can strengthen alliances. They can draw talent from diverse sources, share information and knowledge, and deliver comprehensive services. This chapter discusses the drawbacks to using virtual teams, what is required of their managers, and how leaders can support virtual teams and promote them within the organization and with stakeholders. It describes essential leadership behaviors, necessary organizational changes (e.g., in technology and career-development systems) and structures, and the special challenges that such arrangements create. Finally, it offers a checklist for determining whether an organization is ready to implement virtual teams.

In today's environment organizations must move fast or die. No enterprise, large or small, private or public, can afford to be slow, inflexible, or insular. Powerful market forces, including the rise of e-commerce, are impelling everyone to find new, faster, and more flexible ways of working. At the same time, leaders are seeing that it is no longer necessary—or desirable—for their organizations to own all the assets required to serve customers. Organizations of every size and stripe are focusing on the unique

163

value they can deliver and are finding partners who can provide the expertise or resources to achieve common goals.

With the convergence of these forces, people throughout the enterprise are learning to work with people from outside their office, their organization, even their country. Increasingly they work through virtual teaming. Virtual teams—groups assisted by technology that work across time, distance, and organizational or cultural boundaries—can draw talent from diverse sources, boost returns on intellectual capital, respond more quickly to market opportunities, and facilitate formation of partnerships and alliances.

The nature of these teams, of course, varies with the mission of the organization. Many large private organizations, such as Whirlpool Corporation and Nortel Networks, use virtual teams both inside and beyond the company to create products with worldwide appeal. Other organizations form virtual teams to focus on a single pressing problem. For example, the Consultative Group for International Agriculture Research Centers, a nonprofit agency, has 16 international research centers addressing world hunger. The organization is moving from traditional solo researchers to global, networked project teams.

Many institutions that once worked almost exclusively in the domestic arena are moving toward international virtual partnerships. The National Aeronautics and Space Administration (NASA), for example, has well over 3,000 international agreements on projects ranging from the International Space Station to aeronautics safety. Such collaborations can support projects that one partner could not otherwise fund. Still other organizations use virtual teams to share information and knowledge. The National Child Care Information Center fields teams across the United States that develop and share information on child care, without the benefit of face-to-face contact.

Finally, organizations use virtual teams as the preferred vehicle for delivering services. At IBM, for instance, customer teams partner, communicate, and collaborate on customer problems. Team members are scattered around the world and rarely see each other face to face. They work together every day, however, in electronic "team rooms." INTELSAT, a nonprofit (soon to be for-profit) organization with over 100 international members, uses virtual teams to track satellite position, performance, and capacity for corporate and government agencies.

Virtual Teams Need Real Leaders

Despite the potential benefits, there are many obstacles to working virtually. As distance increases, so do differences in time zones, making same-time communication difficult. Differences in language, culture, and access to technology pose greater challenges. Integration of external partners and alliances requires the integration of work methods, organizational cultures, technology, and goals.

Although communication technology makes virtual arrangements possible, when leaders are asked about their successes and failures with virtual teams, they rarely mention technology as a primary reason for either. Author Bill Davidow, a former executive with Intel and Hewlett-Packard, comments: "Information and communication technology provides an infrastructure . . . to communicate with customers and deliver information necessary for decision making. . . . If management insists on maintaining a purely functional organization or does not empower people, information systems will add little value."

In a world where we may spend more time with the computer than with our colleagues, and may work more closely with partners, contractors, or other outsiders than with members of our own organization, effective leadership is more important than ever. In virtual teams it is the job of broadly dispersed leaders to foster communication and collaboration across distance, time, cultures, and organizational boundaries. Yet many leaders find themselves "accidental virtual leaders" due to mergers, partnership arrangements, or management of ad hoc project teams. They discover they are operating in an environment in which the best management practices of just a few years ago no longer hold. "Management by walking around," for instance, is difficult when we can no longer wander down the hall to see what's happening.

Virtual Team Strategies

Leaders can take several steps, from symbolic actions to targeted changes in work practice, to increase the free flow of information, shared responsibility, and cross-boundary collaboration.

Show that you trust others to work in the best interests of the enterprise. Leaders of effective virtual partnerships recognize that without *trust*, virtual teams cannot function. Almost any attempt to change a system brings unintended consequences, and when you can't see your partner, such consequences are open to negative interpretations. The surest way to build trust is to treat partners as equal: sharing information with them as fully and quickly as possible, including them in decision making, acknowledging their contributions. Especially when working across national boundaries or different cultures, effective leaders create norms and policies about how to do business.

Let them see you act virtually. For virtual teams to succeed, the organization's leadership must establish that virtual teams are not just a fad but a new way of doing business. As Richard

Karl Goeltz, vice chairman and chief financial officer of American Express, notes, "It's important to have a multifunction team of [senior] managers promoting and supporting a virtual office initiative right from the start."

Leaders have at least four ways to demonstrate their commitment (see table). First, they can communicate the business case for new models of work—in part by assigning virtual teams and partners high-profile tasks and projects and then reporting the key benefits and results of their work throughout the organization.

Second, leaders can establish performance standards and expected results. In setting expectations, it is important, for instance, to make clear both the short-term costs and challenges and the long-term benefits of virtual teaming. Such discussions are done openly with all stakeholders and are best held in person.

Third, leaders must allocate resources for training, technology, and travel. They must fight the perception that collaboration is free. It's a mistake, for instance, to think that virtual teams need no travel budget; face-to-face meetings are essential, especially at the beginning of the team's life. Likewise, training in cross-cultural work, project management, and technology takes time and money. Indeed, initially, costs and cycle times may actually increase. Even in Internet time, it can take a while to realize a return on investment.

Fourth, and most important, effective leaders model the behaviors they expect. They align partners as well as cross-functional and regional goals and objectives. They work with other leaders across geographic, organizational, and cultural boundaries. Effective leaders show flexibility, changing as business conditions dictate. They do not expect behaviors from others that they do not engage in themselves.

Managers can support virtual teams in at least four ways.

Communicating	Establishing Expectations	Allocating Resources	Modeling Behaviors
Communicate the business necessity of virtual teams.	Define how virtual teams work and set clear procedures and goals.	Allocate time and money for training for virtual team leaders and members.	Work together on management teams across geographic and cultural boundaries.
Show that virtual team work is respected.	Set high standards for virtual team performance.	Allocate time and money for travel for team leaders for face-to-face meetings.	Solicit input from and display trust in team members.
Discuss the value of diversity and of leveraging skills.	Clarify intended outcomes for customers and other important stakeholders.	Dedicate resources for technology.	Align cross-functional and regional goals and objectives.
Communicate the benefits and results of working virtually.	Factor in start-up costs and times.		Show flexibility.

Essential Leadership Behaviors

Bring People Systems into the 21st Century

Human resource policies and systems must be integrated and aligned to recognize, support, and reward the people who work in and lead virtual teams. The two areas with the most impact on people are career development systems and rewards and recognition.

Career-development systems need to work virtually. Leaders can support virtual team members by providing career opportunities and assignments that are comparable to those in traditional team settings. Virtual team members often mention that they fear that they will be overlooked for promotional opportunities because they are not seen every day. This fear is not unfounded. Managers who lose visual proximity to their employees often put up the strongest resistance to alternative work and team arrangements. Leaders must ensure that the members of virtual teams have the same career development opportunities as the members of traditional teams.

Rewards must be granted for cross-boundary results. In virtual environments, we need to reward what we can't see. Traditional reward and recognition systems favor individual and functional work. Leaders must develop performance objectives for team members that encourage working across boundaries and sharing information.

In addition, incentive systems must be adapted to reward results. In a traditional office environment, where people are seen putting in effort every day, it is possible to reward people for effort as well as for results. In a virtual environment, effort is more difficult to discern. When IBM went to a virtual environment, it also shifted to a reward structure based more on results than effort. The use of formal and informal public recognition of virtual teamwork through on-the-spot awards, bonuses, and other mechanisms can continually reinforce the perception that working virtually is valued. Your organization can use Web-based technology, such as setting up a site for virtual team "best practices" and advertising team successes, as a way to publicly recognize people in a virtual setting.

Balance Structure and Flexibility

Organizational practices need to be clear and flexible to accommodate each team's situation. Most teams, for instance, need straightforward guidelines for accomplishing these tasks:

- Obtaining sponsorship for their activities
- Establishing a project-planning process and identifying intended outcomes
- Estimating and controlling costs
- Documenting work processes
- Reporting results

At an operational level, leaders can also establish preferred systems across working boundaries. For example, many organizations use standard project-management software packages for any team, virtual or on-site. This reduces the time and complexity of starting up, training, and seamlessly linking the teams. Finally, leaders can encourage agreed-on team processes in "soft" areas such as setting team norms, conflict-resolution procedures, and communication protocols for people throughout the organization.

Invest in Teams' Professional Development

The challenges that virtual team leaders face are immense. Many report that they feel as if they are the "glue" that holds the team together. They have to solve problems and build effective working relationships in an environment with little or no face-to-face contact or feedback. These challenges often require us to update fundamental leadership skills. We must learn, for instance, to coach and manage performance without traditional forms of feedback; understand appropriate technologies for electronic communication and collaboration; and cut across organizational barriers to meet the needs of the team. To acquire these new skills, we can seek experience in a variety of virtual teams, find a mentor with these skills (realizing that this person may be our junior), become a mentor to others, or travel or work internationally.

However, every member of a virtual team has to develop new skills as well—including many of the same skills required of their leadership. Leaders can help by encouraging team members to create learning plans and by making strategic use of training and on-the-job assignments. The skills people need will vary, depending on the team's type, mission, and composition. However, most teams require training in six critical areas:

- Project-management techniques
- Networking across functional, hierarchical, and organizational boundaries
- Using electronic communication and collaboration technologies effectively
- Setting personal boundaries and managing time

- Working across cultural and functional boundaries
- Developing interpersonal awareness

Organizational leaders can champion development by providing on-the-job assignments and training that build competence in each area. Assignments that focus on a single important project, cut across organizational boundaries, or involve diverse cultural and functional groups are invaluable.

Make Sure You're Ready for More Than a Fax Machine

Insist on the *appropriate* amount of communication and collaboration technology needed for virtual teamwork. Often less technical solutions will suffice. To profit from more sophisticated solutions such as desktop video conferencing or Internet groupware, you need to have at least three primary organizational conditions in place:

- A well-funded, respected, and established information systems staff, whose members are experienced in installing and supporting electronic collaboration technologies in multiple locations.
- Commitment to keep computer systems as up-to-date as possible, regardless of a person's title or duties. When systems fall behind, the costs of upgrades and the time to introduce them mount quickly. Productivity also may fall as people spend time attempting to fix their equipment or work around it.
- A well-maintained corporate network that has room to expand to meet the needs of more complex systems and users.

If your organization lacks any of these, consider adopting a less complex suite of technologies. In either case, it is important to set technical standards that meet your business's needs and match its mission and strategy. For example, to communicate effectively, a global organization must have audio conferencing equipment, voice mail, fax capability, and access to a common e-mail system. Video conferencing, scheduling, real-time data conferencing, electronic meeting systems, and collaborative writing tools can be added if called for, and if resources exist to make the technology work reliably. You must also have supportive work practices, policies, and philosophies (see "Reality Check: Are You Ready to Go Virtual?").

In developing a communication and collaboration strategy, leaders should also be certain that partners and suppliers have access to compatible technologies if they are considered part of the team. Some organizations have found that partners have very different access to information technology, and the effective use of it depends on the location, culture, and history of the organization.

One leader ran into trouble when her partners in China did not have access to Touch-Tone phones or up-to-date word-processing software. The Chinese were using technology to signify status and intentionally did not upgrade the equipment. Of course, these actions put the Chinese members at a communication disadvantage and damaged productivity.

Our new virtual world is real. We rely increasingly on the work of people outside our enterprise, in diverse functional and organizational roles and with diverse background and expertise. Powerful tools are available to help link us to our partners, collaborators, and customers, but we are only beginning to understand how to use them. We do know, however, that mastering

Reality Check: Are You Ready to Go Virtual?

To assess your organization's readiness for working in virtual teams, mark as many statements as apply. If you mark fewer than four items, proceed with caution; if you mark fewer than three items, consider developing new infrastructure and leadership skills before proceeding at all.

1. Our organization's culture strongly supports cross-boundary work and collaboration at all levels.

2. Our leadership team models virtual teaming and sends clear messages about its importance.

3. Our human resource systems encourage virtual work through career development and rewards and recognition systems.

4. Our organization balances standard yet flexible processes for working in virtual teams.

5. We pay attention to developing people for working virtually.

6. Our organization has the infrastructure to support the level of technology required for virtual work.

the tools and managing the teams through which work is done is not, fundamentally, a question of technology. It is a question of leadership.

Deborah L. Duarte is adjunct professor at George Washington University and international consultant for public, private, and nonprofit sector clients in high technology, retailing, and health care. She is coauthor with Nancy Tennant Snyder of several articles and two books, including *Mastering Virtual Teams*.

Nancy Tennant Snyder is corporate director of change leadership for Whirlpool Corporation and formerly headed the Brandywine Creek Performance Center, Whirlpool's corporate university. She writes and speaks frequently on leadership, collaboration, and technology.

Index